The Pantheon Ancient Rome's best-preserved monument – its ceiling is an amazing feat of engineering *(page 38)*

The Vatican This tiny sovereign papal state stands at the heart of the Roman Catholic world *(page 58)*

Campo de' Fiori Fresh flowers for sale in Rome's most colourful open-air market *(page 44)*

The Roman Forum Imposing ruins mark the hub of the ancient city that ruled a vast empire for centuries *(page 29)*

Villa d'Este Located in the Sabine Hills, it has one of Italy's great gardens *(page 82)*

The Sistine Chapel The awe-inspiring ceiling by Michelangelo is the highlight of the Vatican Museums *(page 68)*

CONTENTS

78

89

51

INTRODUCTION

A ll roads lead to Rome' is not just a figure of speech. In ancient times all routes did indeed radiate from the capital of the Roman Empire. Rome, the Eternal City, was seen as the *caput mundi* – 'capital of the world', ruler of an empire stretching from Gaul and Spain in the west to Egypt and Asia Minor in the east, attracting many different peoples and donating many different legacies to history. But, unlike other comparable cultures that have left a shadow of their former selves, Rome has continued to hold sway. Not only was it an artistic mecca during the Renaissance, and a sanctuary for well-to-do travellers doing the 'Grand Tour' in the 19th century but,

as the centre of Christianity and home of the seat of the Roman Catholic Church from the first Holy Year (1300), it has maintained its cosmopolitan appeal.

Geographically and psychologically, the city is closer to the laid-back south than to the can-do north of Italy. Yet Rome is not a city that stands still. In the 27 centuries of its existence, it has

Roman chariot

seen empires rise and fall, popes and caesars come and go and artistic movements flourish and fade. As a modern European capital, it cannot rest on its laurels. Rome must play the part of an up-to-date political and business city while attempting to preserve its unparalleled cultural heritage.

The Spanish Steps, one of the most popular tourist haunts

Panoply of Treasures

Rome's urban design and architectural history can be closely studied in each phase of development. Take a walk from Trastevere, still locked in a bygone age, through the Centro Storico (historic centre) and you will find that this is one of the most legible cities. The wealth of Rome's patrimony makes most other cities look like paupers. For a start, there are its great ancient remains: the awe-inspiring Pantheon, the imposing Colosseum, the poignant ruins of the Roman Forum. Then there is the cool beauty of the early Christian basilicas and the heritage of medieval Rome, with glorious mosaics and tranquil cloisters. The Renaissance is reflected in elegant churches, graceful palaces and the genius of the artists Raphael and Michelangelo. Finally, the baroque era offers dynamic architecture, theatrical piazzas and flamboyant fountains.

Public Works

Visitors may be bowled over by these treasures, but today's Romans take them in their stride. They are accustomed to conducting their lives against this awesome backdrop, drinking tap water from an aqueduct constructed by a Roman consul and restored by a Renaissance pope. Perhaps Romans take

The Seven Hills

Italy's capital is built on seven hills – Aventine, Capitoline, Caelian, Esquiline, Palatine, Quirinal and Viminale – around the River Tiber, 35km (22 miles) from the sea. The city, the *Comune di Roma*, has a population of approximately 2.6 million and occupies 1,507 sq km (582 sq miles) including the independent city state of the Vatican, which takes up less than half a square kilometre. On the same latitude as New York, Rome has a mild climate, but summers can be hot, so the best time to visit is in spring or early autumn.

Rome too much for granted. While it is refreshing that the city is not treated as an open-air museum, sometimes the locals' apparent indifference to the beauty that surrounds them can be grating. Medieval Romans burned marble statues to obtain lime; modern Romans' love affair with the car does almost as much damage. Fumes and traffic vibration have had a terrible impact on monuments.

However, in the run-up to the year 2000 Jubilee celebrations, the city spent a fortune on a programme of public works designed to enhance the status of the city and restore monuments,

Recalling the glory days

archaeological sites and churches. Museums were revamped, and their hours extended. Church façades were given face-lifts. The main railway station, Stazione Termini, was revitalised and public transport improved, too, with an ever-expanding fleet of mostly new, disability-friendly (and increasingly more ecological or electric) buses. Most traffic has been banned from large areas of the historic centre during the day.

Lastly, a new wave of construction is underway in Rome – a city where for decades it seemed that modern architecture had no place – attracting some of the biggest names in the trade. Former barracks in Rome's northern Flaminio district are being converted by Pritzker prizewinner Zaha Hadid into MAXXI, a national centre of contemporary arts; a museum

Principal Artists and Architects

Bernini, Gian Lorenzo (1598–1680). The foremost exponent of baroque. Works include St Peter's Square, Fountain of the Four Rivers in Piazza Navona, Palazzo Barberini, Galleria Borghese and Santa Maria della Vittoria.

Borromini, Francesco (1599–1667). Baroque architect, assistant to and later rival of Bernini. He designed Sant'Agnese in Agone, Sant'Ivo alla Sapienza and the Palazzo Barberini.

Bramante, Donato (1444–1514). From Urbino, the foremost architect of the High Renaissance created the Belvedere Courtyard in the Vatican Museums.

di Cambio, Arnolfo (circa 1245–1302). Gothic architect and sculptor from Tuscany, his major works are Bonifacio IV's monument and the *ciborium* in St Paul's.

Canova, Antonio (1757–1822). Neoclassical sculptor of Napoleon's sister Pauline in the Borghese Gallery.

Caravaggio, Michelangelo Merisi da (1571–1610). He revolutionised art with bold use of foreshortening, dramatic *chiaroscuro* and earthy realism. His paintings are in Santa Maria del Popolo, San Luigi dei Francesi, Palazzo Barberini, Sant'Agostino, and Galleria Borghese.

Maderno, Carlo (1556–1629). Architect from northern Italy, responsible for the façade of St Peter's and papal palace at Castel Gandolfo.

Michelangelo Buonarroti (1475–1564). Florentine sculptor, architect, painter and one of the great names in the history of art. His creations include the dome of St Peter's Basilica, the Sistine Chapel ceiling, *Moses* in the Church of St Peter in Chains, and the Campidoglio.

Pinturicchio, Bernardino (circa 1454–1513). Tuscan-born painter of frescoes in the Sistine Chapel, the Borgia Apartments and Santa Maria del Popolo.

Raphael (Raffaello Sanzio) (1483–1520). Painter and architect of the High Renaissance. Works include Stanze in the Vatican, Chigi Chapel in Santa Maria del Popolo, and *La Fornarina* in Palazzo Barberini.

centre to house the 9BC Ara Pacis (altar to peace) has been designed by Richard Meier; and Renzo Piano's beautiful music and arts complex, the Auditorium, opened in 2002.

Daily Life

Visitors should not worry about following the maxim of 'when in Rome…' The rhythms of the Roman day will oblige you to do as the Romans do. For instance, you'll soon discover that there is no point in trying to toil round the sights in the summer afternoon heat. This is the time to join the locals seeking the shade of Rome's parks, or else soak up the atmosphere in a piazza, admiring the play of sunlight on russet and ochre façades, listening to the music of the baroque fountains and enjoying one of the refreshing drinks the Romans do so well: perhaps a cool *spremuta d'arancio* made from freshly squeezed oranges, or a creamy *frullato* fruit shake.

The streets begin to thin out after 8pm, and this is your cue to find somewhere to go and eat – and how well you'll eat! Traditional Roman food is based on the cooking of the poor and centres on offal and pasta. Many of the simple, no-frills *trattorie* serving this hearty fare have begun to make way for more sophisticated establishments whose innovative regional Italian cuisine places greater emphasis on experimentation and high quality.

St Peter's, at Rome's heart

Don't feel you have to plan every step in advance. Instead, follow the example of an English aristocrat who came to Rome on his Grand Tour in 1780 and decided to 'straggle and wander about just as the spirit chooses'.

A BRIEF HISTORY

Legend claims that Rome was founded by Romulus, who was sired with his twin brother Remus by the god Mars of a vestal virgin and left on the Palatine Hill to be suckled by a she-wolf. Historians date the founding of the city at 753BC.

Archaeologists have further established that the site was occupied from the Bronze Age, around 1500BC. By the 8th century BC villages had sprung up on the Palatine and Aventine hills, and soon after on the Esquiline and Quirinal ridges. These spots proved favourable since they were easily defensible and lay close to where the Tiber river could be forded. After conquering their neighbours, the Romans merged the villages into a single city and surrounded it with a defensive wall. The marshland below the Capitoline Hill was drained and became the Forum. Under seven consecutive kings, Rome started to become a major force in central Italy.

The Republic

A revolt by Roman nobles in 510BC overthrew the last Etruscan king and established the Republic which was to last for the next five centuries. At first the Republic, under the leadership of two patrician consuls, was plagued by confrontations between patrician (aristocratic) and plebeian (popular) factions. Eventually the plebeians put forward their own leaders, the tribunes, and a solid political order evolved.

In 390BC, the Gauls besieged the city destroying everything but the citadel on the Capitoline Hill. When the Gauls left, the hardy citizens set about reconstructing, this time enclosing their city in a wall of huge tufa blocks. For more than eight centuries, no foreign invader breached those walls.

Rome now extended its control to all of Italy, consolidating its hold with six military roads fanning out from the city –

Appia, Latina, Salaria, Flaminia, Aurelia and Cassia. By 250BC the city's population had grown to 100,000. Victory over Carthage in the Punic Wars (264–146BC) and conquests in Macedonia, Asia Minor, Spain and southern France extended Roman power in the Mediterranean. When Hannibal crossed the Alps and invaded Italy in the Second Punic War, large areas of the peninsula were devastated and peasants sought refuge in Rome, swelling the population still further.

The acquisition of largely unsought territories brought new social and economic problems. Unemployment, poor housing and an inadequate public works programme provoked unrest within the city. Civil wars shook the Republic, which ultimately yielded to dictatorship. Julius Caesar, a former proconsul who had achieved some fame by subduing Gaul and Britain, crossed the tiny Rubicon River, which marked the boundary of his province, and marched boldly on Rome to seize power.

Friends, Romans, countrymen...

Built in the 1st century AD, the Colosseum could seat 50,000

The Empire

Caesar sought to combat unemployment and ease the tax burden, but his reforms bypassed the Senate and he made dangerous enemies. His assassination on the Ides of March in 44BC led to civil war and to the despotic rule of his adopted son Octavian, who, as Augustus, became the first emperor *(see page 52)*. Under Augustus, *Pax Romana* – the peace, or rather the rule of Rome – held together the far-flung Empire. To make Rome a worthy capital, he added fine public buildings in the form of baths, theatres and temples, claiming he had 'found Rome brick and left it marble'. He also introduced public services, including the first fire brigade. This was the Golden Age of Roman letters, distinguished by poets and historians: Horace, Livy, Ovid and Virgil.

In the first centuries of the Empire, tens of thousands of foreigners flooded into Rome, among them the first Christians, including St Peter and St Paul. The emperors tried to suppress this 'new religion', but the steadfastness of its adherents and their willingness to become martyrs increased its appeal.

Each of Augustus' successors contributed his own embellishments to Rome. In the rebuilding after a disastrous fire ravaged the city in AD64, Nero provided himself with an ostentatious villa, the Domus Aurea (Golden House), on the

Esquiline Hill. Hadrian reconstructed the Pantheon, raised a monumental mausoleum for himself (Castel Sant'Angelo), and retired to his magnificent estate, Villa Adriana at Tivoli.

In the late 1st and 2nd centuries AD Rome reached its peak, with a population of over one million. Inherent flaws in the imperial system, however, began to weaken the emperor's power and led eventually to the downfall of the Empire.

After the death of Septimius Severus in AD211, 25 emperors reigned in just 74 years, many of them assassinated. Fire and plague took their toll on the city's population. In 283 the Forum was almost completely destroyed by fire and never recovered its former magnificence.

After a vision of the Cross appeared to him on a battlefield, the story goes, Emperor Constantine I converted to Christianity. He ensured that Christianity was tolerated by an edict passed in 313, and he built the first churches and basilicas in Rome. But in 331 he effectively split the Empire in two when he moved the imperial seat to Byzantium (Constantinople, modern Istanbul). Many of the wealthy as well as talented artists joined him and the old capital never recovered.

The Fall of Rome

Detail of the Arch of Constantine

As the Western Empire went into decline, the Romans recruited northern tribes into the legions to help defend it against other outsiders. But the hired defenders soon deserted, and the disenchanted and weary Roman populace failed to summon up the same enthusiasm to defend the city that they had shown in conquering an empire.

Wave after wave of 'Barbarians' (foreigners) came to sack, rape, murder and pillage: Alaric the Visigoth in 410, Attila the Hun, the Vandals and the Ostrogoths. Finally the Germanic chief Odoacer forced the last Roman emperor, Romulus Augustulus, to abdicate in 476. The Western Empire was at an end, although the Eastern Empire continued until 1453.

Papal Power

In the 6th century, Justinian re-annexed Italy to the Byzantine Empire and codified Roman law as the state's legal system. But, as later Byzantine emperors lost interest in Rome, a new power arose out of the chaos: the papacy. Pope Leo I (440–61) asserted the Bishop of Rome as Primate of the Western Church, tracing the succession back to St Peter who had been martyred in the city. Pope Gregory the Great (590–604) showed statesmanship in warding off the Lombards, a Germanic tribe already established in the north of Italy. In the 8th century, citing a document, the *Donation of Constantine* (later found to be a forgery), the popes began to claim authority over all of Italy.

Pope Gregory the Great from an 11th-century manuscript

Seeking the support of the powerful Franks, Pope Leo III crowned their king, Charlemagne, emperor in St Peter's Basilica on Christmas

Day 800. But the Pope in
turn had to kneel in alle-
giance to the Emperor, and
this exchange of spiritual
blessing for military protection sowed the seeds of future
conflict between the papacy
and secular rulers. Over the

next 400 years, Italy saw invasions by Saracens and Magyars,
Saxons and Normans (who sacked Rome in 1084), with papal
Rome struggling along as only one of many feudal city-states
on the now tormented peninsula. The papacy, and with it
Rome, was controlled by various powerful families from the
landed nobility. As the situation in Rome degenerated into
chaos – deplored by Dante in his *Divine Comedy* – the popes
fled in 1309 to comfortable exile in Avignon, and remained
under the protection of the French king until 1377. Rome was
left to the brutal rule of the Orsini and Colonna families.

The Renaissance

Returning to Rome, the popes harshly put down any resistance
to their rule and remained dominant in the city for the next
400 years. During the 15th and 16th centuries, the papacy became a notable patron of the Renaissance, that remarkable
effusion of art and intellectual endeavour which transformed
medieval Rome from a squalid, crumbling and fever-ridden
backwater to one of the foremost cities of the Christian world.

It was Giorgio Vasari, facile artist and first-rate chronicler
of this cultural explosion, who dubbed this movement a
rinascita, or rebirth of the glories of Italy's Greco-Roman past.
The father of Rome's High Renaissance, Pope Julius II
(1503–13), was responsible for the new St Peter's Basilica. He
also commissioned Michelangelo to paint the ceiling of the Sistine Chapel and Raphael to decorate the Vatican's Stanze.

Donato Bramante, the architect, got the nickname *maestro ruinante* because of the countless ancient monuments he had dismantled for the Pope's megalomaniacal building plans. With the treasures uncovered during this process, Julius founded the Vatican's magnificent collection of ancient sculpture.

But the exuberant life of Renaissance Rome was extinguished in May 1527 by the arrival of the German troops of Holy Roman Emperor Charles V; the last – and worst – sack of the city.

In the mid-17th century, the papacy and the doctrines of the Church of Rome were challenged by Martin Luther, John Calvin and other leaders of the Reformation. A Counter-Reformation was proclaimed in 1563, reinforcing the Holy Office's Inquisition to combat heresy and the Index to censor the arts. Protestants fled and Jews were shut up in a ghetto. Art proved a major instrument of Counter-Reformation propaganda. As the Church regained ground, it replaced the pagan influences of classicism with a more triumphant image, epitomised by Bernini's grand baroque altar canopy in St Peter's. The baroque flourished in Rome as in no other Italian city.

The Habsburgs

In the 18th century, Spain's authority over many of Italy's states passed to the Habsburgs of Austria, who were determined to curb papal power in Rome. The influential order of Jesuits was dissolved, Habsburg church reforms meant a crippling loss of revenue and the papacy lost prestige.

In 1798 Napoleon's troops entered Rome, later seized the papal states and proclaimed a Republic. They treated Pius VI with contempt and carried him off – and many of the treasures of the Vatican – to be a virtual prisoner in France. His successor, Pius VII, was forced to proclaim Napoleon as emperor and for his pains was also made prisoner, returning to Rome only after Napoleon was defeated in 1814.

During the French occupation, a national self-awareness began to develop among Italians to challenge foreign rule. Many looked to Pope Pius IX to lead a nationalist movement, but he feared the spread of liberalism and when a Republic was set up in Rome by Giuseppe Mazzini in 1848, the Pope fled. He returned the following year, after the fall of the Republic.

National unity for Italy was achieved in 1860 through the shrewd diplomacy of Prime Minister Cavour, the heroics of a guerrilla general, Giuseppe Garibaldi, and the leadership of King Vittorio Emanuele of Piedmont. Rome became capital of Italy in 1871 and Pope Pius IX retreated to the Vatican, a 'prisoner of the monarchy'.

Giuseppe Garibaldi monument in Piazzale Garibaldi

The Modern Era

In World War I Italy sided with the allies against Austria and Germany. But after the peace conference of 1919, disarray on the political scene led to an economic crisis, with stagnant productivity, bank closures and rising unemployment. From this turmoil the Fascist movement grew, and when the *fascisti* marched on Rome in 1922, King Vittorio Emanuele III invited their leader, Benito Mussolini *(Il Duce)*, to form a government. Once in power, Mussolini made peace with the

Pope through the Lateran Treaty of 1929, which created a separate Vatican state and perpetuated Roman Catholicism as the national religion. In 1940 Mussolini sided with Hitler in World War II but the Allies declared Rome an open city to spare it from bombing. It was liberated in 1944 with its treasures intact.

Post-War 'Miracle'

The initial post-war period was a time of hardship, but the 1950s saw Rome enjoying Italy's 'economic miracle'. Celebrities made the city their playground, finding *la dolce vita* in the nightspots of the Via Veneto. Rome's population soared, as immigrants from the south came in search of work. Suburbs of blocks of flats shot up on the urban periphery.

In the 1970s, the city weathered a storm of both left- and right-wing political terrorism, and the decade became known as Italy's *anni di piombo* ('years of lead'). The darkest hour came in 1978 when the Red Brigades kidnapped and murdered the former prime minister Aldo Moro.

After the success of the Jubilee year celebrations in 2000, changes to make city services more efficient continue, and authorities are attempting to tackle pollution and traffic congestion, currently the biggest threats to the preservation of the city's rich past. In addition, the number of cultural offerings in Rome has recently increased dramatically, with year-round festivals of every genre, from literature and photography to dance and music, attracting large audiences.

Pope Benedict XVI

Historical Landmarks

753BC Foundation of Rome.

510BC Expulsion of Etruscans. Roman Republic established.

31BC Augustus becomes first Roman emperor.

AD69–79 Emperor Vespasian has the Colosseum built.

98–117 The Empire achieves its greatest expansion under Trajan.

250 First persecution of the Christians under the emperor Decius.

312 Emperor Constantine converts to Christianity and makes Byzantium (Constantinople) the official capital of the Empire.

395 The Empire is divided between West and East.

476 Fall of the Western Roman Empire.

590–604 Pope Gregory the Great establishes new rules for the Church.

800 Charlemagne crowned Holy Roman Emperor.

1309–77 The papacy moves to Avignon, France.

15th century Rome prospers during Renaissance, attracting such masters as Botticelli, Caravaggio, Michelangelo, Raphael and Titian.

1527 Army of Charles V of Spain sacks Rome.

1585–90 Pope Sixtus V commissions Fontana, Bernini, Borromini and Maderno to build churches, palaces, squares and fountains.

17th century The Italian peninsula fragments into numerous smaller states, among them the Papal States, with Rome as their capital.

1801 Under Napoleon, Rome is made part of the French Empire.

1870 Italian troops of the Unification enter Rome, which becomes the capital of the new kingdom of Italy.

1915 Italy joins Allies in World War I.

1922 Mussolini's march on Rome.

1940 Italy joins Germany in World War II.

1944 Rome liberated. King Vittorio Emanuele III abdicates.

1957 Fledgling European Union established under Treaty of Rome.

2002 Lira abolished and euro introduced.

2005 Pope John Paul II dies. Cardinal Joseph Ratzinger is elected Pope Benedict XVI.

2006 Romano Prodi's centre-left coalition narrowly wins the election.

WHERE TO GO

Visitors to Rome soon discover that cultural residues from different eras are often interwoven: a pagan mausoleum is also a papal fortress, a medieval church has a baroque façade, and a Renaissance palace overlooks a modern traffic junction. It doesn't matter whether you've come to Rome for the grandeur of the ancient remains, the revered pilgrimage sites of the Catholic Church or the inspired works of Michelangelo, Raphael and Bernini – you'll end up seeing a glorious hotchpotch of them all.

Although the municipality of Rome sprawls over a huge area, the principal sights are packed into a comparatively small zone. For the most part, the best way of getting about is on foot. Much of the historic centre has been closed to traffic and parking is generally impossible. Rome's public transport has been improved and although crowded during rush hours, it will usually get you near enough to your destination.

> **Closed Mondays**
>
> Many museums are closed on Mondays (the Forum, Colosseum, Palatine and the Vatican museums are notable exceptions) and all are closed on 1 January and 25 December.

PIAZZA VENEZIA AND CAPITOLINE HILL

The most convenient place to begin exploring is **Piazza Venezia**. The hub of the capital's main traffic arteries, this is a principal stop on several major bus routes and close to a number of sites. As far as orientation is concerned, the massive **Il Vittoriano** (Vittorio Emanuele Monument; stairs open daily

Bernini's Fontana del Moro in Piazza Navona

Il Vittoriano, derisively nicknamed but with great views

9.30am–5.30pm, 4.30pm in winter; free) is a landmark visible from all over the city, and provides one of the best views of central Rome. Romans wish the dazzling white marble monument were not quite so conspicuous, however, and heap upon it such derisive nicknames as 'Rome's False Teeth' and 'The Wedding Cake'. Built from 1885 to 1911 to celebrate the unification of Italy and dedicated to the new nation's first king, the Vittoriano contains the **Altare della Patria**, the tomb of Italy's Unknown Soldier of World War I. The monument also has a café, bookshop and a museum complex, with important temporary art exhibitions in its western wing. Once you've climbed to the Altare della Patria, a recently installed lift offers access to a panorama of the city (open Sun–Thur 9am–7.30pm, Fri, Sat 9.30am–1130pm; admission fee; tel: 06-6991718).

A much more impressive work of architecture stands on the west side of the piazza: **Palazzo Venezia**, the first great Renaissance palace in Rome (open Tues–Sun 9am–7.30pm, ticket office closes at 7pm; admission fee). It was once the embassy of the Venetian Republic to the Holy See, and in the 20th century served as Mussolini's headquarters. His desk stood at the far corner of the Sala del Mappamondo, positioned to intimidate visitors, who had to approach across 21m (70ft) of marble floor. From the balcony over the central door in the façade, *Il Duce* harangued crowds in the square below. The palace contains a museum of medieval and Renaissance furniture, arms, tapestries, ceramics and sculpture, and hosts art exhibits.

Capitoline Hill

Two flights of steps lead up behind the Vittorio Emanuele Monument. The more graceful and gradual, **La Cordonata**, takes you up between statues of Castor and Pollux (mythical twin sons of Leda and the Swan) to the tranquil elegance of the **Piazza del Campidoglio** on top of the **Capitoline Hill**.

The First Capitol Hill

To the Romans, the Capitol was both citadel and sanctuary, the symbolic centre of government, where the consuls took their oath and the Republic's coinage was minted. Its name originated when a human skull was unearthed during excavations for the Temple of Jupiter and interpreted as a sign that Rome would one day be head (*caput*) of the world.

When the Gauls sacked Rome in 390BC, the Capitol was saved by the timely cackling of the sanctuary's sacred geese, warning that attackers were scaling the rocks. Later, victorious caesars ended their triumphal processions here. They rode up from the Forum in chariots drawn by white horses to pay homage at the magnificent gilded Temple of Jupiter, which dominated the southern tip of the Capitoline.

In the Middle Ages, the collapsed temples were pillaged and the hill was abandoned to goats until, in the 16th century, Pope Paul III commissioned Michelangelo to give the Campidoglio its new glory.

This was once the Capitol, where the Temple of Jupiter Optimus Maximus Capitolinus stood, ancient Rome's most sacred site. Today the Campidoglio is a fine Renaissance square, designed by Michelangelo (who also designed La Cordonata staircase) for the reception of the Holy Roman Emperor Charles V. Michelangelo also remodelled the existing **Palazzo Senatorio**, Rome's former town hall, and planned the two palaces that flank it, the Palazzo dei Conservatori and the Palazzo Nuovo, which were completed after his death. As a centrepiece, Michelangelo placed the magnificent 2nd century AD bronze **statue of Marcus Aurelius** in the square. According to legend, it was so lifelike that Michelangelo commanded it to walk. The statue you see today is a copy; the original is the star attraction of the newly created glass-covered courtyard in the Musei Capitolini, called the **Giardino Romano**.

Piazza del Campidoglio

The **Musei Capitolini** (open Tues–Sun 9am–8pm; admission fee) in the palaces of the Campidoglio have extensive collections of sculpture excavated from ancient Rome. In the courtyard of the **Palazzo dei Conservatori** (through which you enter the museums) are a giant marble head, hand and foot, fragments from a 12-m (40-ft) statue of Emperor Constan-

Romulus and Remus

tine II. The palace is also home to the *Capitoline She-Wolf* depicted suckling the infants Romulus and Remus. This Etruscan bronze has become the symbol of Rome. In the top-floor **Pinacoteca Capitolina** (Capitoline Picture Gallery) are fine works by Caravaggio, Tintoretto, Velázquez, Rubens and Titian.

An underground passageway lined with artefacts connects the Palazzo dei Conservatori with the **Palazzo Nuovo**. The latter contains rows of portrait busts of Roman emperors, although its highlights are the poignant statue of the *Dying Gaul*, the sensual *Capitoline Venus*, a Roman copy of a Greek original dating from the 2nd century BC, and the *Marble Faun*.

Alongside the Palazzo Senatorio a cobbled road opens out on to a terrace, giving you the best view of the Roman Forum ruins *(see page 29)*, stretching from the Arch of Septimius Severus to the Arch of Titus, with the Colosseum beyond. The steeper flight of steps up the Campidoglio climbs to the church of **Santa Maria in Aracoeli** on the site of the temple of Juno Moneta. The 13th-century church is the home of the much-revered *Santo Bambino* (Baby Jesus), kept in a separate chapel. The original statue, believed to have miraculous powers, was stolen in 1994 and has been replaced by a copy.

ANCIENT ROME

The nucleus of ancient Rome is around the Colosseum *(see page 36)* with the Imperial Fora and Roman Forum to the northwest and the Baths of Caracalla *(see page 37)* to the south. Don't try to decipher each fragment of broken stone – not even archaeologists have succeeded. It's far better to soak up the romantic atmosphere while reflecting on the ruined majesty of this ancient civilisation. Take care to avoid summer's midday sun, as the Forum provides no shade, and finish your visit with a siesta on the Palatine.

The Imperial Fora

Begin at the **Fori Imperiali** (Imperial Fora), which were built as an adjunct to the Foro Romano in honour of Julius Caesar, Augustus, Trajan, Vespasian and Nerva. At the northern end

Trajan's Markets

of Trajan's Forum stands the remarkable 30-m (100-ft) **Trajan's Column** (AD113). Celebrating Trajan's campaigns against the Dacians in what is now Romania, the intricate friezes spiralling round the column constitute a veritable textbook of Roman warfare, featuring embarkation on ships, the clash of armies and the surrender of Barbarian chieftains – in all, using some 2,500 figures. St Peter's statue atop the column replaced the Emperor's in 1587.

Visitor Centre

A Visitor Centre (open daily 9.30am–6.30pm; free) on the Via dei Fori Imperiali between Via Cavour and the Colosseum metro stop gives useful information about the Imperial Fora and ongoing excavation work there. It also runs regular tours in English.

At **Trajan's Forum** (open Tues–Sun 9am–7pm, until 6pm in winter, last entry 1 hour before closing; admission fee) you can see some of the best preserved ancient Roman streets and the semicircular **Trajan's Markets**, an ancient shopping mall, made up of 150 shops and offices. The multi-tiered **Trajan's Forum Museum** (open daily 9am–7.30pm) provides an insight into the history and restoration of the site.

The Roman Forum

You can stand among the columns, porticoes and arches of the **Foro Romano** (open 9am–1 hour before sunset, until 7.30pm in full summer and 4.30pm in winter; free) and, with an exhilarating leap of the imagination, picture the hub of the great Imperial City. Surrounded by the Palatine, Capitoline and Esquiline hills and drained by the Cloaca Maxima, an underground channel, the flat valley of the Forum developed as the civic, commercial and religious centre of the city. Under the emperors, it attained unprecedented splendour, with white marble and golden roofs of temples, law courts and market halls glittering in the sun.

After the Barbarian invasions, the area was abandoned. Subsequent fire, earthquakes, floods and plunder by Renaissance architects reduced the area to a muddy cow pasture, until excavations in the 19th century once again brought many of the ancient edifices to light. Grass still grows between the cracked paving stones of the Via Sacra, poppies bloom among the piles of toppled marble and tangles of red roses are entwined in the brick columns, softening the harshness of the ruins.

Audio-guides can be hired at the entrance on Via dei Fori Imperiali at Piazza Santa Maria Nova 53, or you can find your own way around. Before you begin, make yourself comfortable on a chunk of fallen marble among the ruins and orientate yourself with a detailed map, so that you can trace the layout of the ruins and make sense of the apparent confusion.

Ideally, start at the west end, just below the Campidoglio's Palazzo Senatorio *(see page 26)*. Here you can see how the

The Arch of Septimius Severus and Temple of Saturn

arches of the Roman record office *(Tabularium)* have been incorporated into the rear of the Renaissance palace. Look along the length of the **Via Sacra** (Sacred Way), the route taken by generals as they rode in triumphal procession to the foot of the Capitoline Hill, followed by the legions' standards, ranks of prisoners and carts piled with the spoils of war.

The First Senate House

To counterbalance this image of the Romans as ruthless military conquerors, turn to the brick-built **Curia**, home of the Roman Senate, in the Forum's northwest corner. Here you can gaze through the bronze doors (copies of the originals, which are now in the church of San Giovanni in Laterano; *see page 76)* at the 'venerable great-grandmother of all parliaments', where the senators, robed in togas, argued the affairs of Republic and Empire. The tenets of Roman law, which underpin most European legal systems, were first debated here.

The Curia was constructed in its present form by Diocletian in AD303. Its plain brick façade was once faced with marble. The church that covered it was dismantled in 1937 to reveal an ancient floor set with geometrical patterns in red and green marble, as well as tiers on either side where Roman senators sat, and the brick base of the golden statue of Victory at the rear. The Curia shelters two bas-reliefs, outlining in marble the buildings of the Forum.

In front of the Curia, a concrete shelter protects the underground site of the **Lapis Niger** (usually not on view), a black marble stone placed by Silla over the (presumed) grave of Romulus, the city's founder. Beside it is a stele engraved with the oldest Latin inscription ever found, dating back to the 6th century BC; it has not yet been deciphered.

The triple **Arco di Settimio Severo** (Arch of Septimius Severus) dominates this end of the Forum. Its friezes depict the eastern military triumphs of the 3rd-century emperor

Temple of Castor and Pollux

who later campaigned as far as Scotland. Nearby is the orators' platform, or **Rostra**. Its name comes from the iron prows *(rostra)*, which once adorned it, taken from enemy ships at the Battle of Antium in 338BC. Two points in the Rostra have particular significance: the *Umbilicus Urbis Romae* marks the traditional epicentre of Rome, and the *Miliarium Aureum* (Golden Milestone) recorded in gold letters the distances in miles from Rome to the cities of the far-flung Empire.

Public meetings and ceremonies took place in front of the Rostra, kept bare save for samples of three plants considered sacred to Mediterranean prosperity: the vine, the olive and the fig. Still prominent above this open space is the **Colonna di Foca** (Column of Phocas), built to honour the Byzantine emperor who presented the Pantheon to Pope Boniface IV.

Eight tall columns standing on a podium at the foot of the Capitol belong to the **Tempio di Saturno** (Temple of Saturn), one of the earliest temples in Rome. It doubled as both state treasury and centre of the December debauchery known as the Saturnalia, the pagan precursor of Christmas.

Of the **Basilica Giulia**, which was once busy law courts named after Julius Caesar who commissioned it, only the paving and some of the arches and travertine pillars survive.

Even less remains of the Basilica Aemilia, on the opposite side of the Via Sacra, destroyed by the Goths in AD410.

Three columns, the podium and part of the entablature denote the **Tempio dei Castori** (Temple of Castor and Pollux), built in 484BC. It was dedicated to the twin sons of Leda and the Swan, after they appeared on the battlefield at Lake Regillus to rally the Romans against the Latins and Etruscans.

Caesar's End

The altar of Julius Caesar is tucked away in a semicircular recess of the **Tempio di Giulio Cesare** (Temple of Julius Caesar). On 19 March in 44BC, the grieving crowds, following Caesar's funeral procession to his cremation in the Campus Martius, made an impromptu pyre of chairs and tables and burned his body in the Forum instead.

Pause for a pleasant idyll in the **Casa delle Vestali** (House of the Vestal Virgins), surrounded by graceful statues in the serene setting of a rose garden and old rectangular fountain basins, once more filled with water. In the circular white marble **Tempio di Vesta** (Temple of Vesta), the sacred flame perpetuating the Roman state was tended by six Vestal Virgins, who from childhood observed a 30-year vow of chastity under threat of being buried alive if they broke it. They were supervised by the high priest, the Pontifex Maximus (the popes have since appropriated this title), whose official residence was in the nearby Regia, of which only brick vestiges remain.

Virgin in the Temple of Vesta

The imposing **Tempio di Antonino e Faustina** (Temple of Antoninus and Faustina), further along the Via Sacra, has survived because, like the Curia, it was converted into a church, acquiring a baroque façade in 1602. Few ancient buildings can match the massive proportions of the **Basilica di Massenzio** (Basilica of Maxentius), started by Maxentius and completed by Constantine. Three giant vaults still stand.

The Via Sacra culminates in the **Arco di Tito** (Arch of Titus), built to commemorate the capture of Jerusalem in AD70. Restored by Giuseppe Valadier in 1821, it shows in magnificent carved relief the triumphal procession of Titus bearing the spoils of the city, among them the Temple of Jerusalem's altar, a seven-branched golden menorah and silver trumpets.

The Palatine Hill

From this end of the Forum a slope leads up to the **Palatine Hill** (open 8.30am–7.15pm, 4.30pm in winter; ticket office closes 1 hour earlier; admission fee), Rome's legendary birthplace and today its most romantic garden, dotted with toppled columns among the wild flowers and spiny acanthus shrubs. At the time of the ancient Republic, this was a desirable residential district for the wealthy and aristocratic, including Cicero and Crassus. Augustus began the Imperial trend and later emperors added and expanded, each trying to outdo the last until the whole area was one immense palace (the very word takes its name from the hill). From the pavilions and terraces of the 16th-century gardens laid out here by the Farnese family, there is a superb view of the whole Forum. A small **museum** (follow the signs) displays artefacts found nearby.

The **Casa di Livia** (House of Livia) is now believed to be

Palatine ticket

A ticket for the Palatine Hill includes entry to the Colosseum. Buying your ticket here means you can bypass the lengthy queues at the city's most iconic Roman building (see page 36).

that of her husband, Emperor Augustus, who here combined modesty with taste. Small, graceful rooms retain remnants of mosaic floors. Nearby, three circular Iron-Age dwellings unearthed from the time of Rome's legendary beginnings are known as the **Capanne di Romolo** (Romulus' Huts).

A subterranean passageway, the **Criptoportico** was a secret tunnel linking the Palatine buildings to Nero's palace, the Domus Aurea. In the dim light you can just make out stucco decorations on the ceilings and walls at one end. The vast assemblage of ruins of the Domus Flavia

The Palatine Hill

includes a basilica, throne room, banqueting hall, baths, porticoes and a fountain in the form of a maze. Together with the Domus Augustana, the complex is known as the **Palace of Domitian**. From one side you can look down into the **Stadium of Domitian**, which was probably a venue for horse races.

The last emperor to build on the Palatine, Septimius Severus, carried the imperial palace right to the hill's southeastern end, so that his **Domus Severiana** was the impressive first glimpse of the capital for new arrivals. It was dismantled and its expanses of marble used to build Renaissance Rome.

From this edge of the hill you have a great view down into the immense grassy stretch of the **Circus Maximus**, where vast crowds watched chariot races from tiers of marble seats.

The Colosseum

It says something about the earthiness of Rome that, more than any church or palace, it is the **Colosseum** that is the symbol of the city's eternity (open daily Sept 9am–7pm, 1 Oct–last Sat of Oct 9am–6.30pm, last Sun of Oct–mid-Nov 9am–4.30pm, mid-Feb–mid-Mar 9am–5pm, mid-Mar–last Sat of Mar 9am–5.30pm, end Mar–end Aug 9am–7.30pm; ticket office closes 1 hour earlier; admission fee). Built in AD72–80, the four-tiered elliptical amphitheatre seated some 50,000 spectators on stone benches, according to social status.

The gladiators were originally criminals, war captives and slaves; later, free men entered the 'profession', tempted by wealth and fame. Contrary to popular belief, there is little historical evidence to support the image of the Colosseum as the place where Christians were fed to the lions. Audio-guides for hire at the entrance help bring alive those days.

The Colosseum

Popes and princes stripped the Colosseum of its marble cladding, and its travertine and metal for their churches and palaces. They have left behind a ruined maze of cells and corridors which funnelled men and beasts to the slaughter. The horror has disappeared beneath the moss, but the thrill of the monument's endurance remains. As an Anglo-Saxon prophecy says: 'While stands the Colosseum, Rome shall stand; when falls the Colosseum, Rome shall fall; and when Rome falls, with it shall fall the world.'

The nearby **Arco di Costantino** (Arch of Constantine) celebrates Constantine's victory over his imperial rival Maxentius at Saxa Rubra. He may have won the battle, but a cost-conscious Senate took pieces from monuments of earlier rulers Trajan, Hadrian and Marcus Aurelius to decorate the arch.

Immediately northeast of the Colosseum is the **Domus Aurea** (presently undergoing restoration but partially open for guided tours by appointment only, Tues–Fri 10am–4pm; tel: 06-39967700 for reservations), once a glorious 250-room villa with extensive gardens built by the emperor Nero, who spent very few years in his 'Golden House' before killing himself in AD68. Although extremely interesting for students, archaeologists and art historians, other visitors may be disappointed, as there is very little left of the lavish mosaics, frescoes, inlaid floors and paintings in gold. The last room on the obligatory tour is the octagonal hall with an open skylight and is the most impressive.

Baths of Caracalla

The huge 3rd-century **Terme di Caracalla**, 1km (½ mile) south of the Colosseum, were built for people to bathe in considerable style and luxury (open Tues–Sun 9am–1 hour before sunset; ticket office closes 1 hour earlier; admission fee). Public bathing was a prolonged social event. Senators and merchants passed from the *caldarium* (hot room) to cool down in the *tepidarium* and the *frigidarium*. The baths ran dry in the 6th century when Barbarians cut the aqueducts. Now, in the summer, the baths become the setting for spectacular open-air operas and ballets. Whereas in the past the ruins themselves were used for lighting and stage purposes, in today's more preservation-conscious times, a separate structure is built in the grounds and the ruins serve as a majestic backdrop.

CENTRO STORICO

The heart of Rome's historic centre is the area that is enclosed by the bend of the River Tiber. Here, on what was once the exercise ground of Roman soldiers known as the Campus Martius or 'Field of Mars', you will find vestiges of Rome's many different eras. Next to the remains of ancient temples there is a maze of medieval streets, as well as graceful Renaissance *palazzi*, ornate baroque churches, sublime piazzas and spectacular fountains. But the city centre is up-to-date, too – among the monuments are contemporary shops, hotels and the businesses of modern Rome.

The Pantheon

The magnificent **Pantheon** (open Mon–Sat 8.30am–7.30pm, Sun 9am–6pm; free) in the Piazza della Rotonda is ancient

The Pantheon, temple of all the gods

Rome's best-preserved monument. This 'Temple of All the Gods', and its elegant hemispherical dome that has become a city landmark, was saved for posterity when it was converted into a church in the 7th century. The original Pantheon, built on this site in 27BC by Marcus Agrippa (son-in-law of Augustus), burned down. Emperor Hadrian rebuilt it around AD125, but modest-

The sun looks in through the oculus in the Pantheon's dome

ly left his predecessor's name on the frieze above the portico, which is supported by 16 monolithic pink-and-grey granite columns. The bronze beams that once adorned the entrance were taken away by the Barberini Pope Urban VIII to make Bernini's *baldacchino* canopy for the high altar in St Peter's. His action prompted the saying: '*Quod non fecerunt barbari, fecerunt Barberini*' ('What the Barbarians didn't do, the Barberini did').

The Pantheon's true greatness is only fully appreciated once you step inside and look up into the magnificent coffered **dome**. Over 43m (141ft) in diameter (exactly equal to its height), it is even wider than the mighty cupola of St Peter's Basilica. Held up without any sustaining columns or flying butresses, it is an unparalleled feat of engineering. On fine days a shaft of sunlight illuminates the windowless vault through the circular hole *(oculus)* in the dome (it also lets in the rain). The gods and goddesses are long gone, replaced by the Renaissance tombs of Raphael (and his mistress) and the architect Baldassare Peruzzi, as well as the first king of Italy.

Piazza Navona

A short walk west of the Pantheon is the beautiful **Piazza Navona**, the heart of the northern half of the Centro Storico and a prime spot for recreation since the time of Emperor Domitian, who laid out an athletics arena, Circus Agonalis, on this site in AD79, establishing the future piazza's oval shape.

Jousting tournaments took place here in the Middle Ages, and from the 17th to the 19th century it was the scene of spectacular water pageants in summer, when the fountains overflowed until the piazza was flooded. As bands played, the aristocracy re-enacted the battles of their ancestors, to the delight of thousands of onlookers. Today the piazza remains Rome's perfect stage set, and the public spectacle continues. Secure a front-row seat at any of the alfresco cafés and enjoy the show supplied by artists, performers, musicians and caricaturists, and the people they attract.

The baroque centrepiece of the piazza is Bernini's **Fontana dei Quattro Fiumi** (Fountain of the Four Rivers), which incorporates an ancient obelisk into a monumental allegory symbolising the great rivers of the four continents: the Americas (Río de la Plata), Europe (the Danube), Asia (the Ganges)

Bernini and the Baroque

Although more restrained than elsewhere in Europe, Roman baroque is theatrical, bold and at times bombastic. At the forefront was architect and sculptor, Gian Lorenzo Bernini (1598–1680) whose style found favour with a succession of popes. Even St Peter's is, in part, a Bernini creation, graced by enfolding, keyhole-shaped colonnades. Other masterpieces include the witty design for an elephant to bear the obelisk of Santa Maria sopra Minerva and the angels on Ponte Sant'Angelo. Palazzo Barberini (1629–33) heralded the baroque style and was completed by Bernini, assisted by Borromini, who became his arch-rival.

and Africa (the Nile). Romans who delight in Bernini's scorn for his rivals suggest that the Nile god is covering his head rather than having to look at Borromini's church of Sant'Agnese in Agone, and that the river god of the Americas is poised to catch it in case it collapses. In fact the fountain was completed some years before Borromini's fine façade and dome.

Fountain of the Four Rivers

A brief walk north from the piazza will lead to the **Palazzo Altemps** (open Tues–Sun 9am–7.45pm; ticket office closes 6.45pm; admission fee), a branch of the Museo Nazionale Romano *(see also pages 43 and 74–5)*, which features the magnificent **Boncompagni Ludovisi collection** in a gorgeous 16th-century palace containing frescoed halls, a painted loggia, a church, a theatre and a beautiful internal courtyard. Among the most important pieces is the marble altar top known as the *Ludovisi Throne*, thought to be an original Greek work from the 5th century BC, with exquisitely carved reliefs of Aphrodite and a maiden playing the flute. Also, seek out the tragic *Suicide of a Galatian*, the statue of a Barbarian warrior in the act of killing himself and his wife rather than submit to slavery. Other highlights include the colossal head of Juno and the equally gigantic sarcophagus featuring intricate and highly detailed scenes of battle between Romans and Barbarians. Victory over the Barbarians was a much favoured decorative theme between the second half of the 2nd century AD and the first half of the 3rd century AD.

East of the Pantheon

In an enchanting setting of russet and ochre rococo housing is the 17th-century church of **Sant'Ignazio**. Inside, Fra Andrea Pozzo (himself a Jesuit priest) painted a *trompe l'oeil* **ceiling fresco** (1685) depicting St Ignatius' entry into paradise. Stand on a buff stone disc in the nave's central aisle and look up; you will have the impression of the building rising above you. From any other point, the columns appear to collapse. From another disc further up the aisle you can admire the celestial dome above the baroque altar, but as you advance, the dome begins to take on strange proportions.

South of here, in the Piazza del Collegio Romano, is the main entrance to the vast **Palazzo Doria Pamphili** (also spelt Pamphilj; open Fri–Wed 10am–5pm, ticket office closes at 4.15pm; admission fee; <www.doriapamphilj.it>), the private residence of the important Doria family. The family's rich collection of paintings was assembled over hundreds of years. A catalogue is vital, as paintings are identified only by number.

There are a number of masterpieces from the 15th to the 17th century, including works by Raphael, Titian, Tintoretto, Veronese and Caravaggio, as well as paintings from the Dutch and Flemish schools. Look out for the evocative landscape of the *Flight into Egypt* by Annibale Carracci, Caravaggio's *Penitent Magdalen* and the windswept *Naval Battle in the Bay of Naples* by Brueghel the Elder. You'll find a nice stylistic contrast in a little room off to the side of the galleries: Velázquez's brilliant worldly portrait of Innocent X, the Pamphili family pope, alongside a more serene marble bust of him by Bernini.

Via dei Pastini

The pedestrian-only Via dei Pastini leads east from the Piazza della Rotonda and forms the beginning of a tourist drag that takes in the columns of the Tempio di Adriana, as well as ice-cream outlets and souvenir shops, before crossing the Via del Corso and eventually reaching the Trevi Fountain (see page 52).

South of the Pantheon

Streets on either side of the Pantheon lead south to the Largo di Torre Argentina and across the main road to the **Area Sacra Argentina**, the excavated remains of four temples dating from the 3rd to 1st century BC (viewed from the road only).

At the end of Corso Vittorio Emanuele II to the east is **Il Gesù**, the mother church of the Jesuits and a major element in their Counter-Reformation campaign. Begun as their Roman headquarters in 1568, its open plan became the model for the congregational churches that were intended to wrest popular support from the Protestants. While its façade is more sober than the baroque churches put up subsequently, the interior glorifies the new militancy in bronze, gold, marble and precious stones.

Il Gesù

St Ignatius Loyola, a Spanish soldier who founded the order, has a fittingly magnificent **tomb** under an altar in the left transept, with a profusion of lapis lazuli, a thin shell fused to plaster stucco.

Just south on the Via delle Botteghe Oscure is a recent addition to the Museo Nazionale Romano, the **Crypta Balbi** (open Tues–Sun 9am–7.30pm, ticket office closes 6.45pm; admission fee). Set on the site of the portico of the Imperial Roman Theatre of Balbus, the museum documents the changing faces of Rome through history.

Around the Campo de' Fiori

The hub of the southern section of the Centro Storico is the **Campo de' Fiori**, once the site of public executions during the 17th century, now a lively fruit, vegetable and flower market, one of Rome's most attractive and authentic. A reminder of the square's bloody history, however, is provided by the brooding statue of philosopher Giordano Bruno, who was burned alive during the Counter-Reformation in 1600.

Just south of the Campo is another lovely square, Piazza Farnese. Here, the great architects of the age worked on the **Palazzo Farnese**, Rome's finest Renaissance palace. Begun in 1514 by Antonio da Sangallo the Younger for Cardinal Farnese (Pope Paul III), the project was passed on to Michelangelo, who was responsible for the top floor, and was completed in 1589 by Giacomo della Porta. The building cost so much that it put a great strain on the fortune Farnese had amassed

The bustling market at Campo de' Fiori

while he was treasurer of the Church. The palace is now the French Embassy, and you need special permission to see the dining room's mythological frescoes by Annibale Carracci. Facing Palazzo Farnese, to the left of the square, is **Palazzo Spada** (open Tues–Sun 8.30am–7.30pm; admission fee), a beautiful example of Renaissance art, which houses the art collection of Cardinal Spada in its original setting, including the *trompe l'oeil* trickery of Borromini's famed Perspective Gallery.

Michelangelo's arch, on Via Giulia, near Palazzo Farnese

Nearby, housed in an elegant Renaissance mansion, is the **Museo Barracco** (Corso Vittorio Emanuele 166/A; open Tues–Sun 9am–7pm, ticket office closes 1 hour before closing; admission fee; <http://en.museobarracco.it>). The museum is devoted to ancient sculpture, not just from Rome but from Assyria, Egypt, Cyprus, Phoenicia, Etruria and Greece as well. Highlights of this wonderful collection include works by the Greek sculptor Polyclitus, engraved marble slabs recovered in the Mesopotamian cities of Nineveh and Nimrud, and a head of Heracles from Cyprus.

The Jewish Ghetto

Retrace your steps to the Campo de' Fiori. The narrow streets heading southeast of the marketplace take you into the former **Jewish Ghetto**, a lively and historic district peppered with restaurants serving the city's distinctive Roman–Jewish cuisine. Jews were forced into this confined space in 1555 by Pope

Paul IV. Rules were relaxed considerably after his death, but the walls that confined the quarter were not torn down until 1848. A small but vibrant Jewish community still lives in and around the Via del Portico d'Ottavia. The main synagogue, built in 1904 in the Assyrian-Babylonian style, sits by the river bank and houses a small museum of local Jewish history.

One of the most delightful fountains in Rome, and much loved by children, is the 16th-century **Fontana delle Tartarughe** (Turtle Fountain), in Piazza Mattei. It depicts four boys perched on squirting dolphins while lifting four turtles on to an upper marble basin with gracefully outstretched arms.

Nearby is the **Portico d'Ottavia**, a crumbling, arched façade more than 2,000 years old and dedicated to Augustus' sister. Beyond it extends the **Teatro di Marcello** (Theatre of Marcellus), begun by Julius Caesar, finished under Augustus and said to be the architectural model for the Colosseum.

A short way to the southeast, is the little church of **Santa Maria in Cosmedin**, which was given by the Pope to Rome's Greek colony in the 8th century. Its Romanesque façade and simple interior, with beautiful floor mosaics, provide a stark contrast to the city's dominant baroque grandeur. Test your honesty in the portico's fierce-looking **Bocca della Verità** (Mouth of Truth), made famous by Audrey Hepburn in the 1953 film *Roman Holiday*, on the left wall of the portico. The 12th-century marble face is said to bite off the fingers of anyone putting a hand in the gaping mouth who tells a lie.

Across the road, two of the city's best-preserved temples stand on what was part of the ancient cattle market. The one with 20 fluted Corinthian columns is erroneously known as the **Tempio di Vesta** – probably dedicated to Hercules – and is the oldest standing marble temple in Rome. Its rectangular neighbour, the **Tempio di Fortuna Virile**, is a victim of an ancient typing error, as its presiding deity is believed to have been Portunus, god of harbours, rather than Fortuna (Fortune).

SPANISH STEPS AND TRIDENTE

The city's most sophisticated shopping district, the area around the **Piazza di Spagna** has been attracting foreigners for centuries. Aristocratic travellers on the Grand Tour came here, as did many of the most celebrated artists of the Romantic era, among them Keats, Byron, Balzac, Wagner and Liszt.

The area continues to attract a cosmopolitan crowd. Well-heeled visitors come for the high-fashion boutiques along Via dei Condotti and its grid of neighbouring cobbled streets. The more casually shod linger on the glorious **Scalinata della Trinità dei Monti** (the Span-

ish Steps, named after the nearby residence of the Spanish Ambassador to the Vatican), the city's most popular meeting place for young Romans and foreigners alike. The steps ascend in three majestic tiers to the 16th-century French church of **Trinità dei Monti**. Its twin belfries and graceful baroque façade make it one of Rome's most distinctive landmarks. The steps are adorned with pink azaleas in spring, and in summer they make a spectacular location for occasional designer fashion shows. At Christmas a crib is erected halfway up.

At the foot of the Spanish Steps lies the **Fontana della**

Trinità dei Monti overlooks the Spanish Steps

Barcaccia, a fountain in the shape of a sinking boat. The design, attributed to Pietro Bernini or his far more famous son, Gian Lorenzo Bernini, is an ingenious solution to the problem of low pressure in the Acqua Vergine aqueduct at this point, which supplies this fountain (as well as the Trevi Fountain) with water.

The poet John Keats died of consumption in 1821 at the age of 26 in a small room overlooking the Steps. His house, 26 Piazza di Spagna, has since been preserved as the **Keats-Shelley Museum** (open Mon–Fri 9am–1pm, 3–6pm, Sat 11am–2pm and 3–6pm; admission fee; <www.keats-shelley-house.org>). On the other side of the Steps, at No. 23, **Babington's Tea Rooms** is a pleasant old-world bastion of Anglo-Saxon calm and gentility that has been serving tea and scones since the 1890s.

An even more venerable establishment is on nearby Via dei Condotti. **Caffè Greco** has been a favourite haunt of writers and artists for over two centuries, and the autographed portraits, busts and statues attest to its distinguished patrons,

The Sunday Stroll

A profoundly Italian experience which the leisure-loving Romans excel at is the pre-dinner, or post shop-closing, stroll or *passeggiata*. This is when locals come out on a weekend evening, dressed in their best clothes, to take some air and above all, to see and be seen and, in the case of the younger generation, to eye up their peers and work out who they want to ask out. On Sunday afternoon, locals living in the suburbs spruce themselves up, pile into cars, metros and buses and head for the centre, in particular the pedestrianised Piazza di Spagna, Via del Corso and Piazza del Popolo areas. Once there, they roam the streets at an aimless pace surrounded by relatives of all ages and friends, eating ice creams, exchanging gossip and gazing longingly at shop windows.

among them Casanova,
Goethe, Baudelaire, Buffalo
Bill, Gogol and Hans Christian Andersen. The thick hot
chocolate served here in the
winter by frock-coated waiters is a long-standing tradition among stylish Roman
shoppers and strollers.

Via del Corso

The **Tridente** area takes its
name from the trio of streets

Out to see and be seen

built in the 16th century to relieve congestion in Rome's
cramped medieval centre. Via del Corso, Via di Ripetta and
Via del Babuino emanate like the prongs of a fork from the
Piazza del Popolo, for centuries the main entrance to Rome
for travellers coming from the north.

The **Via del Corso** is the 1.6-km (1-mile) long main street
of central Rome which runs in a straight line from Piazza
Venezia to Piazza del Popolo. Known in ancient times as the
Via Lata, the Corso derives its modern name from the car-
nival races, or *corse*, that were held here in the 15th century
under the spectacle-loving Venetian Pope Paul II. Of all the
races, the most thrilling was the *Corsa dei Barberi*, in which
riderless Barbary horses, sent into a frenzy by saddles spiked
with nails, charged pell-mell along the narrow thoroughfare
to be halted at last by a large white sheet hung across the
street. Today the partly pedestrianised Corso is lined with
palaces and churches and crowded with mainly mid-market
large shops, department stores and shoppers. The streets running off it are full of exclusive boutiques, wineries and cafés.

Roughly halfway along the road is the **Piazza Colonna**,
where the **column of Marcus Aurelius**, decorated with

spiralling reliefs of the Emperor's military triumphs, rises in front of the Italian prime minister's offices in the **Chigi Palace**. The statue of the soldier-emperor that stood on top of the column was replaced in 1589 by one of St Paul.

On the **Piazza Montecitorio** nearby, dominated by a 6th-century BC Egyptian obelisk, is the **Palazzo di Montecitorio**, designed by Bernini for the Ludovisi family. It houses the Camera dei Deputati (Chamber of Deputies), Italy's legislative lower house.

Piazza del Popolo

At its northern, pedestrianised end, the Corso culminates in the graceful oval shape of the **Piazza del Popolo**, a truly exemplary piece of open-air urban theatre, designed in 1818 by Giuseppe Valadier, former architect to Napoleon. The central obelisk, 24m (79ft) high, is from the 13th-century BC Egypt of Ramses II. It was brought to Rome by Augustus and erected in the Circus Maximus. Pope Sixtus V had it moved here in 1589.

The square takes its name from the Renaissance church of **Santa Maria del Popolo**, built at the northern gateway to the piazza on the site of Nero's tomb to exorcise his ghost, reputed to haunt the area. In its baroque interior is a superb fresco of the *Nativity* by the Umbrian painter Pinturicchio in the first chapel on the right, and Raphael's Chigi Chapel, built as a mausoleum for the family of the wealthy Sienese banker and brilliant arts patron, Agostino Chigi. This chapel houses two fine sculptures by Bernini: *Habakkuk* and *Daniel and the Lion*. In the Cerasi Chapel to the left of the altar are two powerful works by Caravaggio, the *Conversion of Saul* and *Crucifixion of St Peter*, notable for the dramatic use of light and shade and the skilful foreshortening of the figures.

The piazza's arched 16th-century **Porta del Popolo** marks the gateway to ancient Rome at the end of the Via Flaminia, which led from Rimini on the Adriatic coast. Pilgrims arriving in Rome by this gate were later greeted by the imposing baroque churches of Santa Maria dei Miracoli and Santa Maria di Montesanto on the southern side, guarding the entrance to the Corso. Two of the most historic and exclusive cafés in Rome, Rosati and Canova, face each other across the expanse.

Pincio Gardens

To the east of the piazza and above the Piazza del Popolo and a monumental complex of terraces, the 19th-century **Pincio Gardens** offer a panoramic view of the piazza

View from Pincio Gardens across Rome to St Peter's

and the city, especially at sunset, when the rooftops are tinged with purple and gold. Also the work of Valadier, the statue-populated gardens occupy the site of the 1st-century BC villa of Lucullus, a provincial governor who returned enriched by the spoils of Asia and impressed his contemporaries by his extravagant lifestyle. The gardens stretch on to the Villa Borghese park *(see page 56)*.

Lined with pine trees and open-air cafés, the Pincio promenade takes you past **Villa Medici**, built in 1564 and bought by Napoleon to house the French National Academy. Today the villa is home to young French artists visiting Rome on scholarships and hosts memorable exhibitions and concerts.

Augustus' Altar of Peace

West of the Via del Corso, towards the banks of the River Tiber is the **Ara Pacis Augustae** (open Tues–Sun 9am–7pm, ticket office closes 6pm; admission fee) in Piazza Augusto Imperatore, a fascinating monument which has been renovated and made into a small museum complex, designed by renowned US architect Richard Meier. After fragments of this 'Altar of Peace', built to celebrate Augustus' victorious campaigns in Gaul and Spain, first came to light in 1568, they were dispersed among several European museums. Most of the pieces were returned to Rome when the building's reconstruction began in the 1930s. The friezes depict Augustus with his wife Livia and daughter Julia, his friend Agrippa and a host of priests and dignitaries. Alongside the altar, the great mound encircled by cypresses is the **Mausoleo di Augusto** (currently closed for restoration), repository of the ashes of the caesars (except Trajan) until Hadrian built his own mausoleum (now the Castel Sant'Angelo, *see page 60)* on the other side of the Tiber.

THE TREVI FOUNTAIN AND QUIRINALE

The **Fontana di Trevi** (Trevi Fountain) never fails to astonish. Nicola Salvi's baroque extravaganza seems a giant stage set, out of all proportion to its tiny piazza. The 18th-century fountain is, in fact, a triumphal arch and palace façade (for the old Palazzo Poli) which frames mythical creatures in a riot of rocks, fountains and pools, all theatrically illuminated at night. The centrepiece is the massive figure of Neptune riding on a seashell

Throw a coin

You must throw a coin into the Trevi Fountain, with your right hand over your left shoulder, to ensure a return to Rome. Donations are made to the Red Cross from the collected coins.

drawn by two winged sea horses led by tritons. The rearing horse symbolises the sea's turmoil, the calm steed its tranquillity. Anita Ekberg and Marcello Mastroianni frolicked memorably in the fountain's waters (carried by an ancient Roman aqueduct) when they starred in Federico Fellini's 1960 film *La Dolce Vita (The Sweet Life)*. Sit on a marble step and enjoy some of the Eternal City's best people-watching.

Quirinale

Between Piazza Barberini and the Imperial Forum, and dominating the summit of the highest of the seven hills

The Trevi Fountain

of ancient Rome, is the baroque **Palazzo del Quirinale** (open Sept–Jun Sun 8.30am–11am; <www.quirinale.it>; admission fee). This was the summer palace of the popes until the unification of Italy in 1870, when it became home to the new king of Italy. Since 1947, it has been the official residence of the president of the Republic. In the centre of the vast Piazza del Quirinale, magnificent **statues of Castor and Pollux** and their steeds, all Roman copies of Greek originals, stand beside an ancient obelisk. Also here is the **Scuderie del Quirinale** (opening hours vary; <www. scuderiequirinale.it>; admission fee), a large space for major exhibitions. The piazza affords a splendid view over the whole city towards St Peter's.

Admirers of the baroque era will find much to delight them in this part of the city, which teems with masterpieces of sculpture and architecture by Bernini. Opposite the *manica lunga* or 'long sleeve' of the Quirinal Palace you will find the small church of **Sant'Andrea al Quirinale**, demonstrating the genius of the 17th-century master in its elliptical plan, gilded dome and stucco work. Further along is the tiny **San Carlo alle Quattro Fontane**, by Bernini's arch-rival, Borromini. It may be small, but with its concave and convex surfaces it is one of Rome's most original church designs.

In the nearby **Piazza Barberini** (at the corner of the Via Veneto) are two of Bernini's celebrated fountains: the **Fontana del Tritone**, which takes centre stage, and the **Fontana delle Api**, on its north side (dedicated to the public and their animals). Both fountains sport the bee symbol taken from the Barberini coat of arms of Pope Urban VIII, Bernini's patron.

The busy genius also had a hand in the architecture of the stately **Palazzo Barberini** (1625–33), which now houses part of the **Galleria Nazionale d'Arte Antica** (open Tues–Sun 9am–7pm, ticket office closes at 7pm; museum is undergoing

Via Veneto

Once the site of a palace surrounded by vast gardens and grounds belonging to the Ludovisi family villa, Via Veneto became renowned in the roaring 1950s and 1960s as the focal point of the so-called *Dolce Vita*, or Hollywood-on-the-Tiber. This twisting avenue lined with elegant and fashionable cafés became the hangout for the rich and famous stars (Audrey Hepburn, James Stewart, Ingrid Bergman and Marcello Mastroianni) working at Rome's Cinecittà film studios, as well as the less famous hoping to be discovered. Though some of the cafés remain, most of the late 19th-century *palazzi* now house impersonal luxury hotels, offices and tourist-orientated restaurants often with tacky, glass-enclosed outdoor seating.

restoration, so only part of it can be visited, for details tel: 06-32810; <www.ticket eria.it>; admission fee). Situated on the Via delle Quattro Fontane, the building provided another architectural battleground for Bernini and rival Borromini, each of whom built one of its grand staircases and contributed to the façade. It is worth a visit as much for its baroque decor as for its collection of 13th- to 17th-century paintings. Don't forget to look up

Bernini's *Ecstasy of St Teresa*

in the *Salone* or **Great Hall** to see Pietro da Cortona's illusionist ceiling fresco, *Triumph of Divine Providence* (1633–9).

Most of the national art collection is hung in the first-floor gallery (the rest is in the Palazzo Corsini across the Tiber in Trastevere). Works include a Fra Angelico triptych, a portrait of King Henry VIII by Hans Holbein and paintings by Titian, Tintoretto and El Greco. Two stars among many are Raphael's *La Fornarina (The Baker's Daughter)*, said to be a portrait of his mistress and model for many of his madonnas, and Caravaggio's depiction of Judith severing the head of Holofernes.

From here, Via Barberini leads to Largo Santa Susanna and the church of **Santa Maria della Vittoria**, home to Bernini's *Ecstasy of St Teresa*, a masterpiece of baroque sculpture.

The Piazza Barberini serves as a base for the **Via Veneto** *(see box opposite)* that heads north from here to the park of the Villa Borghese. Home to embassies, deluxe hotels and outdoor cafés, Via Veneto is now only faintly evocative of the days when Rome was the hedonistic Hollywood of Europe.

VILLA BORGHESE

At the top of Via Veneto, across Piazzale Brasile, is the large and leafy **Villa Borghese** park, once the estate of Cardinal Scipione Borghese, the nephew of Pope Paul V. The grounds contain the Galleria Borghese in the cardinal's former summer palace; a collection of modern art in the former Orangery; and Italy's finest Etruscan art collection in the Villa Giulia.

Galleria Borghese and Museo Carlo Bilotti

The avid and ruthless art collector Cardinal Scipione Borghese conceived this handsome baroque villa on the eastern side of the park as a home for his small but outstanding collection, using his prestige as the nephew of Pope Paul V to extort coveted masterpieces from their owners.

Temple on Villa Borghese's lake

Galleria Borghese (open Tues–Sun 9am–7pm, entry is every two hours from 9am–5pm; booking essential; tel: 06-32810; <www.galleriaborghese.it>; admission fee) is one of Italy's best small museums. The highlights are astonishing **sculptures** by the cardinal's young protégé, Bernini. These include busts of his patron, a vigorous *David* and a graceful sculpture, *Apollo and Daphne*, in which the 26-year-old sculptor depicts the water nymph turning into a laurel just as the god is about to seize her. But the gallery's star attraction is Antonio Canova's portrayal of Napoleon's sister Pauline, who married into the Borghese family, as a reclining Venus (1805). Exceptional

Villa Borghese park

Villa Borghese park is not only great for a gentle stroll; you can hire bicycles and rollerblades in the grounds, or take a rowing boat out on the picturesque lake.

pieces include Raphael's *Deposition*; Titian's *Sacred and Profane Love*; a number of Caravaggio's works, including *David with the Head of Goliath* and the *Madonna of the Serpent*; along with works by Botticelli, Cranach, Dürer and Rubens.

The former Orangery of Villa Borghese has been transformed into the **Museo Carlo Bilotti** (Viale Fiorello La Guardia; open Tues–Sun 9am–7pm; admission fee), which houses a collection of modern and contemporary art.

Villa Giulia

This 16th-century pleasure palace built for Pope Julius III in the northwest area of the Villa Borghese park, is now the setting for Italy's finest **Etruscan Museum** (open Tues–Sun 8.30am–7.30pm, ticket office closes 1 hour earlier; admission fee). Although much about this pre-Roman civilisation is still a mystery, the Etruscans (found in Tuscany, Umbria and in parts of Lazio, north of Rome) left a wealth of detail about their customs and everyday life by burying the personal possessions of the dead with them in their tombs. Replicas show the round stone burial mounds, built like huts. Room after room is filled with objects from the tombs: bronze statues of warriors; shields, weapons and chariots; gold and silver jewellery; decorative vases imported from Greece; and a host of everyday cooking utensils, mirrors and combs. The highlight is a life-size terracotta 6th-century BC sculpture for a sarcophagus lid, depicting a blissful young couple on a banquet couch.

Looking down from the basilica over St Peter's Square

THE VATICAN

The power of Rome endures both in the spirituality evoked by St Peter's Basilica and in the awe inspired by the splendours of Vatican City. At their best, the popes and cardinals replaced military conquest by moral leadership and persuasion; at their worst, they could show the same hunger for power and wealth as any caesar or grand duke.

Constantine, the first Christian emperor, erected the original St Peter's Basilica in 324 over an oratory on the presumed site of the tomb of the Apostle, who was martyred (with St Paul) in Rome in AD67. After it was sacked in 846 by Saracens, Pope Leo IV ordered walls to be built around the church, and the enclosed area was known as the Leonine City, and then Vatican City, after the Etruscan name of its location.

The Vatican became the main residence of the popes only after 1378, when the papacy was returned to Rome from exile in Avignon. It has been a sovereign state, independent of Italy, since the Lateran Pact signed with Mussolini in 1929. The Pope is supreme ruler of this tiny state, which is guarded by an elite corps of Swiss Guards, founded in 1506, who still wear the blue, scarlet and orange uniforms said to have been designed by Michelangelo. The papal domain has its own newspaper, *L'Osservatore Romano*, and a radio station which broadcasts worldwide. It also has shops, banks, a minuscule railway station (rarely used) and an efficient postal service that issues its own Vatican stamps.

Apart from the 1 sq km (0.4 sq mile) comprising St Peter's Square, St Peter's Basilica, and the papal palace and gardens, the Vatican also has jurisdiction over extraterritorial enclaves, including the basilicas of San Giovanni in Laterano, Santa Maria Maggiore and St Paul's, as well as the Pope's summer residence at Castel Gandolfo, to the southeast of the city.

You don't need a passport to cross the border, which you may not even notice – though it is marked by a band of white travertine stones running from the ends of the two colonnades at the rim of St Peter's Square. The **Vatican Tourist Information Office** on the south side of St Peter's Square arranges guided tours and issues tickets to Vatican City, including the gardens. From here you can reach the Vatican Museums on foot in 15 minutes. A visit to St Peter's combines well with a tour of Castel Sant'Angelo, but it's best to save the Vatican Museums for a separate day: their 7km (4 miles) of galleries are best savoured in small doses.

A Swiss Guard in a uniform designed by Michelangelo

Ponte Sant'Angelo and castle

Castel Sant'Angelo

Cross the Tiber by the **Ponte Sant'Angelo**, which incorporates arches of Hadrian's original bridge, the Pons Aelius, built in AD134. Ten angels carved by Bernini and his studio between 1598 and 1660, each bearing a symbol of the Passion of Christ, adorn the balustrades.

From the bridge you have the best view of **Castel Sant' Angelo** (open Tues–Sun 9am– 7pm, ticket office closes 6pm; admission fee), its mighty brick walls stripped of their travertine cladding and pitted by cannonballs. Conceived by Hadrian as his family mausoleum, it became part of the defensive Aurelian Wall a century later. The castle gained its present name in AD590 after Pope Gregory the Great had a vision of the Archangel Michael alighting on a turret and sheathing his sword to signal the end of a plague. For centuries this was Rome's mightiest military bastion and a refuge for popes in times of trouble; Clement VII holed up here during the sack of Rome by Habsburg troops in 1527.

A spiral ramp, showing traces of the original black-and-white mosaic paving, leads up to the funerary chamber where the ashes of emperors were kept in urns. You emerge into the **Cortile dell'Angelo** (Courtyard of the Angel), which is stacked neatly with cannonballs and watched over by a marble angel. An arms museum opens off the courtyard.

After the grimness of the exterior, it comes as a surprise to step into the luxurious surroundings of the old **Papal Apartments**. Lavish frescoes cover the walls and ceilings of rooms hung with masterpieces by Dosso Dossi, Nicolas Poussin and Lorenzo Lotto. Off the Courtyard of Alexander VI is the most exquisite bathroom in history. Just wide enough for its marble tub, it is painted with delicate designs over every inch of its walls and along the side of the bath.

A harsh jolt brings you back to reality as you enter the **dungeons**, scene of torture and executions. You have to bend over double to get into the bare, stone cells where famous prisoners languished – among them sculptor-goldsmith Benvenuto Cellini and philosopher and monk Giordano Bruno.

The **Gallery of Pius IV**, surrounding the entire building, affords a panoramic view, as does the terrace on the summit, with the 18th-century bronze statue of *St Michael* by Verschaffelt. Opera lovers will recall this as the setting for the final act of Puccini's *Tosca*, in which the heroine hurls herself to her death from the battlements.

St Peter's Basilica

From Castel Sant'Angelo, a wide, straight avenue, the Via della Conciliazione, leads triumphantly up to St Peter's. A maze of medieval streets, where Raphael had a studio, was destroyed in 1936 by Mussolini's architects to provide an unobstructed view of St Peter's all the way from the banks of the Tiber. A thick wall running parallel to the avenue

Entering eternity

The poet Goethe once said that entering St Peter's is 'like entering eternity'. The world's largest Roman Catholic church certainly has immense dimensions: 212m (695ft) long on the outside, 187m (613ft) inside, and 132m (433ft) to the tip of the dome. Brass markers on the floor of the central aisle show how far other famous cathedrals fail to measure up.

conceals a passageway *(Il Passetto)* linking the Vatican to the Castel Sant'Angelo, for fleeing popes to reach their bastion.

In **Piazza San Pietro** (St Peter's Square), Bernini's greatest creation, is one of the world's most exciting pieces of architectural orchestration. The sweeping curves of the colonnades reach out to embrace Rome and draw pilgrims into the bosom of the Church. On Easter Sunday as many as 300,000 people cram into the piazza to hear Mass. The square is on or near the site of Nero's Circus, where early Christians were martyred.

Bernini completed the 284 travertine columns and 88 pilasters topped by 140 statues of the saints in 11 years, from 1656–67. In the centre rises a 25-m (82-ft) red granite **obelisk**, brought here from Egypt by Caligula in AD37. Stand on one of the two circular paving stones set between the obelisk and the twin 17th-century fountains to see the quadruple rows of perfectly aligned Doric columns appear magically as one.

Seeing the Pope

When he is in Rome, it is possible to see the Pope at his personal residence, the Vatican. He normally holds a public audience every Wednesday at 10am in a large modern audience hall. An invitation to a papal audience may be obtained from the Prefecture of the Pontifical House by letter or fax (Prefettura della Casa Pontificia, 00120 Città del Vaticano, tel: 06-69884857, fax: 06-69885863), or by going directly to their offices in St Peter's Square any weekday morning from 9am–1pm. In high season you should book a few weeks in advance. From the end of July to early September the papal audience is held at Castel Gandolfo.

On Sundays at noon, the Pope appears at the window of his apartments in the Apostolic Palace (to the right of the basilica, overlooking the square), delivers a homily, says the Angelus, and blesses the crowd below. On a few major holy days, the pontiff celebrates High Mass in St Peter's and may make an appearance on the basilica's open balcony.

A grandiose achievement, **St Peter's Basilica** (open daily 7am–7pm in summer, until 6pm in winter; free; no bare legs or shoulders) nevertheless suffers from the competing visions of its master architects, who included Bramante, Carlo Maderno, Michelangelo and Raphael. Each added, subtracted and modified, often with a pope peering over his shoulder.

Michelangelo's dome

From 1506, when the new basilica was begun under Julius II (replacing the original church built in the 4th century by Constantine), until 1626 when it was consecrated, St Peter's Basilica changed form several times. It started out as a simple Greek cross, with four arms of equal length, as favoured by Bramante and Michelangelo, and ended up as Maderno's Latin cross, extended by a long nave, as demanded by the popes of the Counter-Reformation. One result is that Maderno's porticoed façade and nave obstruct a clear view of Michelangelo's dome from the square.

Michelangelo's Masterpiece

The basilica's most worthy artistic treasure, Michelangelo's **Pietà** (1500), is in its own chapel to the right of the entrance. The artist was 25 when he executed this moving marble sculpture of the Virgin cradling the crucified Christ in her lap. It is the only work that he signed (on the ribbon that crosses the Madonna's breast), after overhearing people crediting it to another sculptor. Since the statue was attacked by a religious fanatic with a hammer in 1972 (a chunk of the Virgin's nose was broken off and an eyelid chipped, but the damage was

Michelangelo's *Pietà*

immediately restored), it has been protected by bulletproof glass. Reverence can also cause damage: on the 13th-century bronze statue of St Peter the toes of the right foot have been worn away by the lips and caressing fingers of pilgrims over the centuries.

Beneath the dome, Bernini's great *baldacchino* (canopy) soars over the high altar, at which the Pope celebrates Mass. The canopy and four spiralling columns were cast from bronze beams taken from the Pantheon. At the foot of each column a coat of arms bears the three bees of the Barberini Pope Urban VIII, who commissioned the work. In the apse is another extravagant baroque work, Bernini's bronze and marble Cathedra of St Peter, into which the wooden chair of the saint is supposedly incorporated. Also by Bernini is the tomb of Urban VIII.

For his imposing **dome** (open 8am–6pm, until 5pm in winter; admission fee), Michelangelo drew inspiration from the Pantheon and Brunelleschi's cupola on Florence's cathedral. A lift takes you as far as the gallery above the nave, which gives a dizzying view down into the basilica, as well as close-ups of the inside of the dome. Spiral stairs and ramps lead up to the outdoor balcony which encircles the top of the dome for stunning views of St Peter's Square, Vatican City and all of Rome.

The **Vatican Grottoes** beneath the basilica contain the tombs of popes and numerous little chapels. The **necropolis**, even deeper underground, shelters pre-Christian tombs, as well as a simple monument which marks St Peter's alleged burial place. This excavated area is not open to general viewing and visits should be arranged in advance through the Ufficio Scavi (Excavations Office, just beyond the Arco della Campana to the left of the basilica, email: scavi@fsp.va).

Masses are said in the side chapels, in various languages.

The Vatican Museums

It should come as no surprise that the Roman Catholic Church, the world's greatest patron to painters, sculptors and architects, should have in its headquarters one of the richest art collections in the world. The **Vatican Museums'** 7km (4 miles) of rooms and galleries offer a microcosm of Western civilisation (open Mon–Fri 8.45am–4.45pm, Sat 8.45am–2.45pm in summer, Mon–Sat 8.45am–1.45pm in winter, 8.45am–1.45pm last Sun of the month, ticket office shuts 85 minutes before closing; <www.vatican.va>; admission fee – free entry last Sun of the month). There is a bewildering profusion to see here, from Egyptian mummies, Etruscan gold jewellery and Greek and Roman sculpture, to medieval and Renaissance masterpieces to modern religious art.

Inside the Vatican's galleries

With the booty from the ruthless dismantling of ancient monuments to make way for the Renaissance city in the 16th century, the **Museo Pio-Clementino** has assembled a wonderful collection of classical art. The most celebrated piece is the 1st century BC *Laocoön* group: the Trojan priest and his two sons who were strangled by serpents sent by the goddess Athena for refusing to allow the Greek horse to enter Troy. Famous during Imperial times, it was unearthed from a vineyard on the Esquiline Hill in 1506, to the delight of Michelangelo, who rushed to view it. It now stands in a recess of the octagonal Belvedere Courtyard.

Roman copies of some other Greek sculptures, such as the *Aphrodite of Cnidos* by Praxiteles and the *Apollo Belvedere*, achieved a fame as great as the lost originals. In particular, note the powerful, muscular, 1st-century BC *Torso* by Apollonius, which has had a profound influence on artists and sculptors to this day.

Giuseppe Momo's staircase

The **Museo Etrusco** holds the finds from a 7th-century BC Etruscan burial mound at Cerveteri *(see page 85)*, whose tomb yielded an abundance of treasures. Among the fine jewellery is a gold brooch curiously decorated with lions and ducklings. Look out for the bronze statue of a sprightly Etruscan warrior, the *Mars of Todi*, from the 4th century BC.

Judging by the number of obelisks scattered throughout the city, Egyptian art was much sought after by the ancient Romans. The basis of the collection in the **Museo**

Egiziano rests on finds from Rome and its surroundings, particularly from the Gardens of Sallust between the Pincian and Quirinal hills, the Temple of Isis on the Campus Martius and Hadrian's Villa at Tivoli *(see page 82)*. One room recreates the underground chamber of a tomb in the Valley of the Kings.

The Raphael Rooms

Pope Julius II took a calculated risk in 1508 when he called in a relatively untried 26-year-old to decorate his new residence. The result was the four **Stanze di Raffaello** (the Raphael Rooms). In the central and most visited Stanza della Segnatura are the two masterly frescoes, *Disputation over the Holy Sacrament* and the famous *School of Athens*, which contrasted theological and philosophical wisdom. The *Disputation* unites biblical figures with historical pillars of the faith such as Pope Gregory, Thomas Aquinas and others, including painter Fra Angelico and the divine Dante. At the centre of the *School*, Raphael is believed to have given red-robed Plato the features of Leonardo da Vinci, while portraying Michelangelo as the thoughtful Heraclitus, seated in the foreground. Raphael himself appears in the lower right-hand corner.

For a stark contrast to Raphael's grand manner, seek out the gentle beauty of Fra Angelico's frescoes in the **Cappella del Beato Angelico** (Chapel of Nicholas V). The lives of saints Lawrence and Stephen are told in delicately subdued pinks and blues, highlighted with gold.

The six richly decorated halls of the **Borgia Apartments** contain Pinturicchio's frescoes, with portraits of the Spanish Borgia Pope Alexander VI and his notorious son Cesare and daughter Lucrezia, and leads into the **Collection of Modern Religious Art** opened in 1973 by Paul VI. Among the 20th-century works are Matisse's Madonna sketches, Rodin bronzes, Picasso ceramics, designs for ecclesiastical robes and, somewhat unexpectedly, a grotesque pope by Francis Bacon.

One of Europe's finest collections of ancient manuscripts and rare books is held in the **Apostolic Library**. In the great reading room, or Sistine Hall, designed by Domenico Fontana in 1588, walls and ceilings are covered with paintings of ancient libraries, conclaves, thinkers and writers. Showcases holding precious manuscripts have replaced the old lecterns. A 1,600-year-old copy of Virgil's works, the poems of Petrarch, a 6th-century gospel of St Matthew and Henry VIII's love letters to Anne Boleyn are among the prized possessions.

The Sistine Chapel

Nothing can prepare you for the shock of the **Cappella Sistina** (Sistine Chapel), built for Sixtus IV in the 15th century. Restored in a 20-year project that finished in 1994, the brightness and freshness of the frescoes are overwhelming. At the time some art critics claimed that the frescoes had been cleaned

The *Creation of Adam* in Michelangelo's Sistine Chapel

beyond recognition and had lost their original tonality. Be that as it may, visitors seem to yield to the power of Michelangelo's ceiling and his *Last Judgement*. The other wall frescoes, by Botticelli, Ghirlandaio, Pinturicchio, Rosselli and Signorelli, are barely acknowledged. In this private papal chapel, where cardinals hold their conclaves to elect new popes, the glory of the Catholic Church achieves its finest artistic expression.

The chapel portrays the biblical story of man, in three parts: from Adam to Noah; the giving of the Law to Moses; and from the birth of Jesus to the Last Judgement. Towards the centre of the ceiling you will be able to make out the celebrated outstretched finger of the *Creation of Adam*. Most overwhelming of all is the impression of the whole. This is best appreciated looking back from the bench by the chapel's exit.

On the chapel's altar wall is Michelangelo's tempestuous *Last Judgement*, finished 25 years after the ceiling's completion in 1512, when the artist was in his sixties. An almost naked Jesus dispenses justice; he is more like a stern, classical god-hero than the conventionally gentle biblical figure. It is said that the artist's agonising self-portrait can be seen in the flayed skin of St Bartholomew, below Jesus.

The Picture Gallery

Amid all the Vatican's treasures, the 15 rooms of the **Pinacoteca Vaticana** (Picture Gallery) in a separate wing, sometimes get short shrift. Covering nine centuries of painting, there are important works by Fra Angelico, Perugino, Raphael's *Transfiguration*, Leonardo da Vinci's unfinished *St Jerome*, Bellini's *Pietà* and Caravaggio's *Descent from the Cross*. As you wander the galleries, glance out of the windows to view St Peter's dome over the Vatican Gardens (the best views are from the Gallery of the Maps). Take a rest in the **Cortile della Pigna**, dominated by the bronze pine-cone fountain (1st century AD) which gives the courtyard its name.

Santa Maria in Trastevere

TRASTEVERE, THE AVENTINE & TESTACCIO

The Ponte Fabricio, one of Rome's oldest bridges (62BC), links the left bank to the tiny **Isola Tiberina** (Tiber Island). Three centuries before Christ the island was the sacred property of Aesculapius, god of healing, to whom a temple and hospital were dedicated. The large **Fatebenefratelli** hospital, originally founded in 1548 by the friars of St John of God, stands here to this day, occupying most of the island. A second bridge, Ponte Cestio, remodelled in the 19th century, leads over to the river's right bank and the neighbourhood of Trastevere.

Trastevere

Trastevere, 'across the Tevere (Tiber)', has been Rome's traditional working-class quarter since ancient times, and its inhabitants pride themselves on being the true Romans. Despite recent gentrification that has dotted the district with smart shops, tearooms, clubs and restaurants, Trastevere retains a lively, idiosyncratic character, particularly in the cobbled streets around Piazza di Santa Maria in Trastevere.

The church of **Santa Maria in Trastevere** is reputedly the oldest in the city. Its foundation can be traced to the 3rd century AD, but the present structure dates from 1130–43 and is the work of Pope Innocent II, himself a *Trasteverino*. The façade is decorated with a beautiful 13th-century mosaic of the Virgin flanked by 10 maidens bearing lamps. The highlight of the interior are undoubtedly the 12th-century Byzantine mosaics covering the floor and apse.

Before entering **Santa Cecilia in Trastevere**, pause in the courtyard of the church to admire the russet baroque façade and endearingly leaning Romanesque tower (AD1113). Now regarded as the patron saint of music, St Cecilia was martyred for her Christian faith in AD230. Her chapel stands over the site of her home and *caldarium* (the bathhouse, still visible) in which she was tortured by scalding; she was finally beheaded when these attempts didn't work. The sculptor Stefano Maderno was on hand when her tomb was excavated in 1599 and his beautiful statue shows the miraculously conserved body that served as his model.

The **Gianicolo** (Janiculum Hill) can be reached from Trastevere by following the long and winding Via Garibaldi uphill. After the liberation of Rome from papal rule in 1870, this hill became a gathering place where anticlerical citizens could honour Giuseppe Garibaldi. A large equestrian monument to the freedom-fighter stands on Piazzale Garibaldi and, a little further north, is another for his wife, the intrepid Anita. The views

'We others'

Noantri, dialect for 'we others', reflects the way the *Trasteverini* see themselves. It is also the name of their festival of music, food and fireworks in the last two weeks of July.

The Tempietto

Bramante's Tempietto is one of the finest examples of High Renaissance architecture. Set in an Early Renaissance courtyard, it possesses a gravity all of its own – marking the alleged site of St Peter's crucifixion.

from the terrace are magnificent. Also on the hill is **San Pietro in Montorio**, with works by Vasari, del Piombo and Bernini. Bramante's **Tempietto**, one of the gems of the Renaissance, was erected in the courtyard in 1502.

The Aventine

Revered in ancient times as the 'Sacred Mount', when it stood outside Rome's walls, the **Aventine Hill** remains a quiet sanctuary above the clamour of the city. An aristocratic district in the Imperial era, the hill is still a favoured residential zone, with villas and apartments set in shady gardens.

The Aventine is also the site of some of the earliest Christian churches, the most beautiful of which is the basilica of **Santa Sabina** built around AD425. The 24 white Corinthian columns lining the nave give the church a classic harmony, while the beautiful carved 5th-century cypress-wood doors in the portico contain one of the earliest depictions of the crucifixion. Through an atrium window you can see a descendant of an orange tree planted by St Dominic in 1220. A few steps away stands the villa of the **Cavalieri di Malta** (Knights of Malta). Peep through the keyhole of the closed garden gates for a perfectly framed view of the dome of the distant St Peter's, a favourite post-card subject.

Testaccio

Just below the genteel residential slopes of the Aventine Hill lies the bustling neighbourhood of **Testaccio**, traditionally working-class and now on the rise. The **Mattatoio** (open Tues–Sun 9am–7pm; <www.macro.roma.museum>; admission fee), was a slaughterhouse until 1975. These days, part of the complex hosts a (somewhat distant) wing of the MACRO contemporary art museum; technically called MACRO Future, commonly referred to as MACRO Mattatoio. Prestigious international exhibitions – including some massive installations – take advantage of this unusual exhibition space. There's a busy nightlife scene in Testaccio, with some of the most authentic *trattorie* in Rome and a growing array of chic wine bars and delis.

For something more tranquil, head to Porta San Paolo, where dark cypresses shade the beautiful **Cimitero Acattolico** (Protestant Cemetery; open Mon–Sat 9am–5pm), where John Keats was buried in 1821 and where the ashes of his friend Shelley were interred the following year. Towering over the cemetery is Rome's only **pyramid**, which has survived because it was incorporated in the city walls. A colonial magistrate, Caius Cestius, commissioned the 30-m (100-ft) monument for his tomb in 20BC on his return from Egypt.

Pyramid of Caius Cestius

MONTI AND ESQUILINO

On the western side of the Esquiline Hill lies the large *rione* (neighbourhood) of **Monti**, encompassing the Fori Imperiali and two major basilicas: Santa Maria Maggiore and San Giovanni in Laterano. In the hilly, leafy streets between Via Panisperna and Via Cavour, it has retained interesting traces of its medieval past, as well as an intimate village feel. On the other side of the hill is Piazza Vittorio Emanuele II, the focal point of the **Esquilino** *rione*, a truly multi-racial area, with many ethnic food shops and an interesting market selling fresh produce, clothes and domestic goods on Via Lamarmora.

The Baths of Diocletian

Diocletian's Baths and Palazzo Massimo

Part of the Museo Nazionale Romano, the **Terme di Diocleziano** (open Tues–Sun 9am–7.45pm, ticket office closes 6.45pm; admission fee) offer a good introduction to Rome's Greek and Roman antiquities. Larger even than those of Caracalla, Diocletian's Baths covered 120 hectares (300 acres), part of which are now occupied by the Piazza della Repubblica and the church of Santa Maria degli Angeli, near the Termini station.

The largest part of the Museo Nazionale Romano collection is housed in the nearby 19th-century **Palazzo Massimo** (opening times as above), including frescoes taken from the imperial villa of Livia. These show nature at its most bountiful, with flowers, trees, birds and fruit painted with great attention to detail (visited only as part of a guided tour). There is also an impressive collection of statues and busts of emperors, their relatives and lovers, and mythological creatures. Highlights include the *Niobid* statue from the Gardens of Sallust, the seated bronze *Pugilist* or Boxer, and the *Sleeping Hermaphroditus*. There are also collections of ancient Roman jewellery, as well as coins from the Republic and Imperial eras up until the Renaissance.

Santa Maria Maggiore

Southeast of the Piazza della Repubblica is the Basilica of **Santa Maria Maggiore** (open daily 7am–7pm; free). According to a 13th-century legend, this largest and most splendid of all the churches dedicated to the Virgin Mary was built in the 4th century by Pope Liberius after a vision from the Virgin Mary. In fact, the church almost certainly dates from 420, and was completed soon afterwards by Pope Sixtus III.

Glittering **mosaics** enhance the perfect proportions of the interior. Above the 40 ancient Ionic columns of the triple nave, a mosaic frieze portrays Old Testament scenes leading to the coming of Christ. The theme is continued in the gilded Byzantine-style mosaics on the triumphal arch, detailing the birth and the childhood of Jesus, and culminates in the magnificent 13th-century portrayal of Mary and Jesus enthroned in the apse behind the high altar. Inlaid red and green precious marbles pattern the floor in a style pioneered by Rome's illustrious Cosmati family of craftsmen during the 12th century.

Just south of Piazza Cavour is the 5th-century **San Pietro in Vincoli**, built as a sanctuary for the chains with which Herod bound St Peter in Palestine. It contains one of Michelangelo's greatest sculptures, ***Moses***, which was intended for

St Peter's as part of the sculptor's unsuccessful project for Julius II's tomb. *Moses* was going to be just one of 40 figures adorning the tomb, but the plan was aborted when Julius decided he wanted Michelangelo to paint the Sistine Chapel instead.

San Giovanni in Laterano

Situated in a large piazza to the southeast of the Colosseum is the mother church of the Roman Catholic world (seat of the Pope as Bishop of Rome), **San Giovanni in Laterano**, which predated the first St Peter's Basilica by a few years. Popes lived in the Lateran Palace for 1,000 years until they moved to Avignon, and then to the Vatican on their return in 1377.

Fire, earthquake and looting by Vandals reduced the church to ruins over the centuries. The present structure uses the bronze central doors that once graced the entrance to the Curia in the Forum in ancient Rome. High above the basilica's façade, 15 giant white statues of Jesus, John the Baptist and Church sages stand against the sky.

Transformed by Borromini in the 17th century, the sombre interior is more restrained than is usual for baroque architects. The only exuberant touches are the coloured marble inlays of the paving and statues of the Apostles. The **baptistery**, site of the first Christian baptism in Rome, preserves some 5th- to 7th-century mosaics. Brothers Jacopo and Pietro Vassalletto excelled themselves in the **cloisters**, where alternating straight and twisted columns, in mosaic style, are a perfect setting for meditation.

An ancient edifice opposite the basilica – almost all that's left of the original Lateran Palace – shelters the **Scala**

Ancient obelisk

Outside San Giovanni in Laterano stands an obelisk brought from the Temple of Ammon in Thebes. It is the tallest in the world – 32m (102ft) – and, dating from the 15th century BC, very possibly the oldest of the 13 still standing in Rome.

Santa, the stairway brought back by St Helena from Jerusalem and said to have been trodden by Jesus in the house of Pontius Pilate. The devout still climb the 28 marble steps to the **Sancta Sanctorum** ('Holy of Holies', the private chapel of the popes; admission fee) on their knees.

San Clemente

On the Via San Giovanni in Laterano stands a gem of a church, which hides a fascinating history within its three levels. In its present basilica form, **San Clemente** dates from the 12th century, with three naves divided by ancient columns and embellished by

San Clemente

a pavement of geometric designs. A symbolic mosaic in the apse features the Cross as the Tree of Life nourishing all living things: birds, animals and plants. To the right of the nave, a staircase leads down to the 4th-century **basilica**, which underpins the present church. The Romanesque frescoes, unfortunately, have drastically faded, but copies show the near-perfect condition in which they were uncovered early in the 20th century.

An ancient stairway leads deeper underground to a maze of corridors and chambers, believed to be the home of St Clement himself, third successor to St Peter as Pope and martyred by Hadrian in AD88. Also here is the earliest religious structure on the site, a 2nd-century AD pagan **temple** *(Mithraeum)* dedicated to the god Mithras.

FURTHER AFIELD

Via Appia Antica

Don't miss a visit to the **Via Appia Antica**, the Old Appian Way, just outside the city walls. Heading southeast through the Porta San Sebastiano, look back for a good view of the old **Aurelian Wall**, still enclosing part of Rome. Its massive defensive ramparts stretch into the distance, topped by towers and bastions built to resist the onslaught of Barbarian invasions in the 3rd century. Ahead lies a narrow lane, hemmed in at first by hedges and the high walls of film stars' and millionaires' homes – the Old Appian Way. When the Censor Appius Claudius opened the consular road and gave it his name in 312BC, the Appian Way was the first of the great Roman roads. You can still see some of the original paving stones over which the Roman legions marched 370km (222 miles) on their way to Brindisi to set sail for the Levant and North Africa.

By law, burials could not take place within the city walls, so on either side of the road lie the ruins of sepulchres of 20 generations of patrician Roman families, some with simple tablets, others with impressive mausoleums.

The Old Appian Way

At a fork in the road, the 17th-century chapel of **Domine Quo Vadis** marks the spot where St Peter, fleeing Nero's persecution, is said to have met Christ and asked: '*Domine, quo vadis?*' ('Whither goest thou, Lord?'). Christ is believed to have replied: 'I go to Rome to be crucified again.' Ashamed of his fear, Peter turned back to Rome and his own crucifixion. The chapel contains a copy of a stone with a footprint said to be that of Jesus (the original is in the Basilica of San Sebastiano).

The Catacombs

Further along the Appia Antica, within a short distance of each other, are three of Rome's most celebrated **catacombs**: San Domitilla, San Callisto (the largest and the most famous) and San Sebastiano. Millions of early Christians, among them many martyrs and saints, were buried in 50 of these vast underground cemeteries. Guides accompany groups into a labyrinth of damp, musty-smelling tunnels and chambers burrowed into the soft volcanic tufa rock, sometimes six levels deep. Early Christian paintings and carvings adorn the catacombs.

San Domitilla is the oldest and perhaps the most enjoyable to visit (open Feb–Dec Wed–Mon 9am–noon, 2–5pm in summer, until 5pm in winter; admission fee). The entrance to the **Catacombs of San Callisto** lies at the end of an avenue of cypresses (open Mar–Jan Thur–Tues 9am–noon, 2–5pm, until 5pm in winter, ticket office closes 30 minutes earlier; admission fee). An official tour takes you down to the second level of excavations, where you will see the burial niches, or *loculi*, cut into the rock one above the other on either side of the dark galleries. Occasionally the narrow passages open out into larger chambers, or *cubicula*, where a family would be buried together. More than 10 early popes were buried here. In the **Catacombs of San**

The Circus of Maxentius

Sebastiano (open mid-Dec–mid-Nov Thur–Tues 9am–noon, 2–5pm, closed Wed; admission fee), the bodies of the apostles Peter and Paul are said to have been hidden during the 3rd-century persecutions.

Near the Catacombs of San Callisto is the poignant memorial of **Fosse Ardeatine**, which has become a place of pilgrimage for modern Italians. In March 1944, in retaliation for the killing of 32 German soldiers by the Italian Resistance, the Nazis rounded up at random 335 Italian men (10 for each German and an extra 15 for good measure) and machine-gunned them in the sandpits of the Via Ardeatina.

The cylindrical **Tomb of Cecilia Metella** (open Tues–Sat 9am–6.30pm; admission fee) dominates the Appian landscape. This noblewoman was the wife of the immensely rich Crassus, who financed Julius Caesar's early campaigns. The well-preserved **Circus of Maxentius**, built for chariot races in AD309, extends alongside.

Further south is the 2nd-century **Villa dei Quintili** (entrance at Via Appia Nuova 1092; open Tues–Sun 9am–1 hour before sunset; admission fee), the Quintili brothers' sumptuous residence, with a bath complex and nymphaeum, and the **Parco degli Acquedotti**, dotted with the remains of Roman aqueducts.

Ostiense

South of Testaccio lie the Ostiense and Garbatella quarters, filled with striking late 19th- and early 20th-century workers' apartment blocks. Once industrial, **Ostiense** is becoming more gentrified, offering some of Rome's hippest nightlife.

In a former electricity power plant a 10-minute walk from Testaccio's pyramid is one of Rome's must-see sights that appeals to all ages. The **Centrale Montemartini** (Via Ostiense, 106; open Tues–Sun, 9am–7pm, ticket office closes at 6.30pm; tel: 06-5748030; admission fee) has been converted into a fascinating museum which juxtaposes industrial machinery with more than 400 classic Roman statues.

Between Via Guglielmo Marconi and the Tiber lies **San Paolo Fuori le Mura**. Originally built by Constantine in AD314 and enlarged by Valentinian II and Theodosius, St Paul's was Rome's largest church after St Peter's. It stood intact until razed by fire in 1823, but was faithfully restored.

Massive Byzantine doors in 11th-century bronze panels survived the fire and now appear on the west wall. A **ciborium** (1285) attributed to the Florentine architect and sculptor Arnolfo di Cambio decorates the high altar, under which lies the supposed burial place of St Paul the Apostle.

Above the 86 Venetian marble columns runs a row of mosaic medallions representing all the popes, from St Peter to the present day. A main feature is the peaceful Benedictine **cloister** from the early 13th century.

A 'Third Rome'?

Beyond the ancient and modern city, a 'Third Rome' exists 5km (3 miles) south along the Ostian Way. A complex of massive white-marble buildings, EUR was designed for a world fair in 1942 to mark 20 years of Fascism. War halted construction, and the fair never took place. Recently, EUR has developed into a thriving township of government ministries, offices and apartments.

EXCURSIONS

Tivoli and the Sabine Hills

The picturesque town of **Tivoli** perches on a steep slope amid the **Sabine Hills**. Inhabited even in ancient times, when it was known as *Tibur*, Tivoli prospered throughout the Middle Ages. It preserves interesting Roman remains, as well as medieval churches and its famous Renaissance villa.

COTRAL buses connect Rome to Tivoli from the Ponte Mammolo metro station (line B). Not all the buses stop at Villa Adriana. By car the drive takes 45 minutes on Via Tiburtina; or take the A4 Autostrada towards Aquila and exit at Tivoli.

Villa d'Este, Villa Adriana and Villa Gregoriana

The **Villa d'Este** sprawls along the hillside (open Tues–Sun 8.30am–1 hour before sunset; <www.villadestetivoli.info>; admission fee). From its balconies you can survey its fabled gardens, which fall away in a series of terraces – a paradise of cypresses, umbrella pines, fountains (some 500) and statues.

Cardinal Ippolito II d'Este conceived this modest villa and garden in 1550; architect Piero Ligorio created it. On the **Viale delle Cento Fontane** water jets splash into a basin guarded by statues of eagles. The **Fontana dell'Organo**, originally accompanied by organ music, cascades steeply down the rocks. The architect took delight in strange fantasies, such as the rows of sphinxes who spurt water from their nipples.

Down the road (5km/3 miles), tucked away at the foot of the hills, lie the ruins of **Villa Adriana** (Hadrian's Villa; open Nov–Jan 9am–5pm, Feb 9am–6pm, Mar and Oct 9am–6.30pm; Apr and Sept 9am–7pm, May–Aug 9am–7.30pm, ticket office closes 1 hour earlier; admission fee). Spread over 70 hectares (173 acres), this retirement hideaway of the Emperor Hadrian was one of the most extravagant constructed in ancient times.

You enter the ruins through the colonnades of the Greek-style **Pecile** (a pool which was once surrounded by a portico), which leads to the imperial residence. Adjoining the palace are guest rooms, their mosaic floors visible, and an underground passageway through which servants moved about.

The **Teatro Marittimo**, a pavilion surrounded by a reflecting pool and circular portico, epitomises all the magic of the place. To the south, remnants of arches and copies of Greek-style caryatids (statues of females used as pillars) surround the **Pool of Canopus** leading to the sanctuary of the Egyptian god Serapis. Barbarians and museum curators have removed most treasures, but a stroll among the arches, pillars and mosaics evokes a lost world. Two museums recreate the retreat in its day.

Villa d'Este

Villa Gregoriana (open Tues–Sun 10am–6.30pm, till 2.30pm in winter; admission fee; <www.villagregoriana. it>), in the centre of Tivoli, is an oasis of waterfalls, ravines and grottoes. In 1826 the river Aniene burst its banks and swept away much of the town. Architect Clemente Folchi duly diverted the river, boring into the mountainside to create a series of spectacular waterfalls. Colour-coded walks lead off from the main waterfall, ending up at the **Temple of Vesta**, a round, travertine structure dating back to the 1st century BC.

Ostia Antica

Excavations continue to uncover fascinating sections of what was once the seaport and naval base of Rome when it was the most important city in the Western world. The long-buried city of **Ostia** stands at the mouth *(ostium)* of the Tiber, 23km (14 miles) southwest of the capital on the shores of the Tyrrhenian Sea. Sea-going vessels were unable to travel inland along the shallow Tiber, so river barges plied back and forth from the port, carrying imperial Rome's supply of food and building materials. During its heyday, the port city had 100,000 residents, two splendid public baths, a theatre (where plays are still occasionally offered), many temples and wealthy villas.

Exploring Ostia Antica

Ostia's ruins (open Apr–Oct Tues–Sun 8.30am–7pm, Nov–Feb Tues–Sun 8.30am–5pm, Mar 8.30am–6pm, ticket office closes 1 hour earlier; admission fee), set among cypresses and pines (perfect for picnics), may reveal more about daily life and the building methods of ancient Rome than do those of the capital. Excavations since the 19th century have unearthed **Decumanus Maximus** (Main Street) and a grid of side streets lined with warehouses, apartments known as *insulae* and private houses which face the sea and are decorated with mosaics and murals.

The **Piazzale delle Corporazioni** (Square of the

Guilds) housed 70 commercial offices around a porticoed central temple to Ceres, goddess of agriculture. Mosaic mottoes and emblems in the pavement tell of the trading of grain factors, caulkers, ropemakers and shipowners from all over the world. The **theatre** next door, built by Agrippa, is worth the climb up the tiered seats for a view over the whole ruined city.

As in Rome, the **Forum** was the focus of city life, dominated at one end by the Capitol, a temple dedicated to Jupiter, Juno and Minerva, and at the other by the Temple of Rome and Augustus, with the Curia (seat of the municipal authorities) and the basilica, or law courts, lying in between.

To see a typical residence, visit the **House of Cupid and Psyche** with its rooms paved in marble and built round a central garden courtyard. Nearby a small on-site **museum** traces Ostia's history through statues, busts and frescoes.

The 1930s resort of **Lido di Ostia** attracts weekending Romans. The sea is not very clean here, but it is lined with *stabilimenti* (beach clubs), many of which have restaurants and pools. There are some sections of *spiaggia libera* ('free beach', without a fee) and at night bars open up on the beach.

Cerveteri

The **Etruscan necropolis** at Cerveteri, 43km (27 miles) northwest of Rome, was in ancient times *Caere*, one of the 12 towns of the powerful Etruscan League, which declined in the 3rd century BC after becoming a Roman dependency (open Tues–Sun 8.30am–1 hour before sunset; admission fee). The scores of **tombs** here represent every kind of burial, dating from the 7th to 1st century BC. Decorations and carvings depict the things that Etruscans felt they needed in the afterlife. The **Museo Nazionale Cerite**, housed in a 16th-century castle in Piazza Santa Maria, displays a collection of objects from the tombs (open Tues–Sun 8.30am–7.30pm; free).

WHAT TO DO

SHOPPING

Italian fashions and products from its gifted artisans are extremely popular and it's not unusual to buy a suitcase to take home the goodies. The small, traditional shops are fun to browse. Real bargains can be found in January and July sales.

IVA (value-added tax) is incorporated into prices on a sliding scale, reaching 20 percent. Non-EU citizens are entitled to a refund of this tax on purchases of €155 or more, if made in one place; ask for an invoice from the seller. Save receipts until you leave your last EU destination. If you are leaving from Rome, take your receipts to be stamped *before* you check in. Watch for shops with a sign, TAX-FREE SHOPPING FOR TOURISTS, which usually deduct the IVA on the spot. For more information visit <www.globalrefund.com>.

Where to Shop

The most fashionable (and expensive) shopping district lies between Piazza di Spagna and Via del Corso. The best in high fashion, jewellery, fabrics and leather is available in elegant shops on Via dei Condotti and its side streets: Via Borgognona, Via Frattina and Via Bocca di Leone. Stroll from Piazza di Spagna to Piazza del Popolo on Via del Babuino for other famous-name boutiques. Streets branching from Campo de' Fiori are good for quirky fashion and artisans' boutiques and workshops.

Via Cola di Rienzo, just across the river, is not so exclusive but its stores offer good, sometimes excellent quality. Via Nazionale and Via del Tritone are less expensive places for both fashionable clothes and leather.

The latest trends on the Via del Corso

An artisan at work

The best of Rome's big stores are Coin (Piazzale Appio, near San Giovanni in Laterano) and La Rinascente (main branch at Piazza Colonna on Via del Corso). The Standa and Upim chains, with branches throughout the city, are good for essentials.

Be prepared to haggle at Porta Portese, Rome's famous flea market held on Sunday morning in tiny streets parallel to Viale Trastevere between Porta Portese and Piazza Ippolito Nievo in Trastevere. You will find clothes, furniture, bric-à-brac, jewellery and books.

The outdoor market in Via Sannio (near San Giov-anni in Laterano) has bargain clothes (Mon–Fri 8.30am–1.30pm, Sat till 6pm). Between Via G. Pepe and Via Mamiani, in a former barracks, is Nuovo Mercato Esquilino, Rome's most colourful and multicultural food and clothes market.

What to Buy

Antiques. Dealers by the score sell exquisite (but expensive) silver, glass, porcelain, furniture and paintings. The best shops are on Via del Babuino and Via Margutta (between the Spanish Steps and the Piazza del Popolo), Via Giulia (behind Palazzo Farnese) and Via dei Coronari (near Piazza Navona). Buy only from a reputable dealer, who will provide a certificate of guarantee and obtain a government export permit.

Books and prints. The open-air market at Largo Fontanella Borghese (off Via del Corso) specialises in prints and books. Ceramics: Leone Limentani (Via del Portico d'Ottavia 47) has a wealth of ceramics, with discounts on discontinued lines.

Fashion. All the famous names of Italian *alta moda* (high fashion) are represented in the Piazza di Spagna area. Fendi and Valentino are Rome's local stars, but you'll find all their peers as well: Armani, Etro, Krizia, Prada, Missoni, Versace, Gucci and Max Mara. You'll also find tailored men's clothes, both custom-made and ready-to-wear.

Food and wine. Delicacies include Parmesan, salami, Parma and San Daniele ham *(prosciutto crudo* – meat products cannot be taken to the US), extra virgin olive oil, Castelli Romani wines and fiery *grappa*. Ai Monasteri in Corso Rinascimento (off Piazza Navona) sells liqueurs, confectionery, olive oil and other products made by Italian monasteries. Trimani (Via Goito 20) is the city's most historic wine shop (since 1821).

Interior design. Showrooms worth visiting include Spazio Sette (Via dei Barbieri 7) located in a 17th-century former cardinal's palace. For the latest in lighting head for Artemide (Via Margutta 107) and Flos (Via del Babuino 84).

Jewellery. You'll find modern, antique and costume jewellery. Bulgari in Via dei Condotti for opulence, or the stores on Via del Governo Vecchio – particularly Tempi Moderni (No. 108) – for vintage and costume jewellery.

Chic leather bags and belts

Leather. Stylish shoes, handbags, gloves, wallets and luggage abound. Furla, on Piazza di Spagna, sells fashionable and affordable bags.

ENTERTAINMENT

Rome offers a wealth of evening entertainment, especially in summer when balmy evenings entice everyone outdoors. Rome's summer festival, the *Estate Romana*, runs from June to September and offers music, film, dance, theatre and much more in venues across the city (<www.estateromana.it>).

Music Venues

The best venue for **classical and contemporary music** is the Auditorium Parco della Musica (Viale Pietro de Coubertin 30, tel: 06-80241281, <www.auditorium.com>), with a large outdoor amphitheatre, three indoor halls and exhibition spaces. Bus M runs from Stazione Termini every 15 minutes directly to the Auditorium. The renowned Accademia di Santa Cecilia (<www.santacecilia.it>) and its symphonic and chamber orchestras host their main concerts at the Auditorium from October to May. Classical music is also performed in picturesque and historic settings, such as the Campidoglio (see *page 25*), the beautifully frescoed Oratorio del Gonfalone and the cloister of Santa Maria della Pace. Outdoor venues include Villa Ada, Teatro di Marcello and Villa Celimontana.

Booking Ahead

There are a few central booking services for advance purchase of tickets for major sights and museums. This eliminates the need to queue in high season. **Pierreci** (tel: 06-39967700, <www.pierreci.it>) handles the Colosseum, Roman Forum, Baths of Caracalla and other ancient sites in and outside Rome. **Ticketeria** (tel: 06-32810, <www.ticketeria.it>) covers the Galleria Borghese, Palazzo Barberini and many others. For theatres, concerts, sporting events, etc, try **Orbis** (Piazza dell'Esquilino 37, tel: 06-4827403, <www.helloticket.it>).

Opera and ballet performances are presented at the Teatro dell'Opera (Piazza Beniamino Gigli near Via Torino, tel: 06-48160255, <www.operaroma.it>). The opera season runs from November to late spring, with ballet the rest of the year. In July and August the troupe perform a selection of operas and ballets outdoors in the highly evocative Baths of Caracalla.

Street entertainment

Music clubs abound, from jazz, blues and folk to rock, reggae and salsa. Major live venues are Alexanderplatz (Via Ostia 9, tel: 06-39742171, <www.alexanderplatz.it>) and La Palma (Via G. Mirri 35, tel: 06-43599029, <www.lapalmaclub.it>). Blues and jazz are found at Trastevere's Big Mama (Vicolo San Francesco a Ripa 18, tel: 06-5812551, <www.bigmama.it>).

Cinemas usually dub foreign films into Italian. Exceptions are the Alcazar (on Mondays) and the Nuovo Olimpia (near the Spanish Steps). The Metropolitan (just off Piazza del Popolo) and Warner Village Moderno (near Piazza della Repubblica) also show original-language films on one screen.

For information about what's going on in Rome, consult the daily newspapers, the entertainment supplement, *Trovaroma*, in the Thursday edition of *La Repubblica* newspaper and *Roma C'è*, which comes out on Wednesdays. *L'Evento*, a monthly guide to events in and around the city, is available from Rome's Tourist Information Points *(see page 126)*. Sometimes even major events aren't confirmed until close to the last minute: see also <www.romaturismo.it> for updated events.

CHILDREN'S ROME

Children love Rome's fountains, the Bocca della Verità *(see page 46)*, the catacombs *(see page 79)* and horse and carriage rides around the city (find them in Piazza di Spagna or in Piazza Madonna di Loretto, off Piazza Venezia). On the pedestrianised Piazza Navona there are all sorts of diverting performers and other street-life entertainment. Also on the piazza are two Roman **toy shop** institutions – Al Sogno (No. 53) and Bertè (No. 107). Nearby, at Via Della Scrofa 65, is another excellent toy shop called Città del Sole.

A favourite with the city's children is the **Villa Borghese park** *(see page 56)*. Here entertainments include pony-rides and a merry-go-round (near Porta Pinciana), bicycle and rollerblade hire (near the Pincio), and a boating lake (near Piazza di Siena). Rome's zoo is also tucked away in a corner and now referred to as **Bioparco** due to its increasingly animal-friendly outlook. Villa Borghese is large and sprawling so ask for directions or get a map at the tourist office before venturing off.

For the under 12s, the children's museum, **Explora** (open Tues–Sun 10am–7pm, hours vary, entry is about every 2 hours

Gelaterie are never far away

until 5pm; call first to check, tel: 06-3613776, <www.mdbr. it>), is at Via Flaminia 82, a 10-minute walk from Piazza del Popolo. Laid out like a small city with hospital, shops and post office, it's a place where children can touch, observe and play.

Don't forget the many *gelaterie*, selling ice cream in multiple flavours; cones begin at about €1.50–2.

Festivals and Events

1 January New Year's Day. Public holiday.

6 January *Befana* (Epiphany). Festival in Piazza Navona. Public holiday.

17 January Blessing of the animals at Sant'Eusebio, Via Napoleone III.

February/March *Carnivale*. The period preceding Lent with masked processions and parades.

9 March *Festa di Santa Francesca Romana*. Blessing of cars by the patron saint of motorists, Monastero Oblate di Santa Francesca Romana, Via Teatro di Marcello 32.

March/April Easter weekend. Pope leads the Stations of the Cross *(Via Crucis)* on Good Friday from 9pm onwards at the candlelit Colosseum. On Easter Sunday the Pope blesses the crowds from the balcony of St Peter's at noon. Easter Monday is a public holiday.

April–May Cultural Heritage Week. Free admission to state museums and monuments. *Festa della Primavera*. Spring Festival, azaleas on the Spanish Steps. Five-day open-air art exhibition in Via Margutta.

21 April Anniversary of the legendary founding of Rome, celebrated with an evening of fireworks.

25 April Liberation Day. Public holiday.

1 May *Festa del Lavoro*. Labour Day, free rock concert usually held in the square in front of the basilica of San Giovanni in Laterano. Public holiday.

29 June *Festa di San Pietro e San Paolo*. Solemn rites in St Peter's Square.

July *Noantri*. Two-week long festival in Trastevere with music, food, street theatre, stalls and fireworks.

5 August *Festa della Madonna della Neve* in Santa Maria Maggiore.

15 August *Ferragosto* (Feast of the Assumption). Public holiday.

October Five-day open-air art exhibition in Via Margutta.

1 November *Ognissanti* (All Saints' Day). Public holiday.

2 November All Souls' Day. Romans visit family graves.

December Christmas market and fair on Piazza Navona (until 6 January).

8 December *Festa dell'Immacolata Concezione*. Public holiday.

24–26 December Christmas Eve midnight Mass celebrated by the Pope in St Peter's Basilica. 25 and 26 December are Christmas holidays.

EATING OUT

For Italians, sitting down at the table and enjoying a meal together has always been a celebration. They like to spend hours at the table, chatting with their family and friends and drinking wine. Now that non-residents' traffic has been banned from large sections of Rome's historic centre, outdoor dining can be a delight. The area around Campo de' Fiori *(see page 44)* and nearby Piazza Navona *(see page 40)* has become what Via Veneto was during the days of *la dolce vita* – a place to while away the evening, first at one of the many restaurants and later at an outdoor café. Other dining spots are Trastevere *(see page 70)* and the old Jewish Ghetto *(see page 45)*.

Restaurants must display the menu with prices in the window or just inside the door. By law all restaurants must also issue a receipt *(ricevuta)* indicating the name, address and VAT number of the premises. The bill usually includes service (called either *servizio* or *coperto*), but ask if you're not sure.

Where to Eat

Some hotels, usually the larger ones, serve an English-style breakfast. Otherwise, go to any local bar or café and ask for a *caffè* (black espresso coffee) or *cappuccino* (with foaming hot milk), accompanied by a delicious sweet *cornetto* (croissant). Remember that in a bar you will pay at least double if you sit down and are given waiter service instead of consuming any beverages (and food) standing up at the bar *(al banco)*.

For a quick snack at lunchtime, choose a *tavola calda*, a bar with informal tables serving a variety of hot and cold dishes to take away or eat on the spot. Many bars offer the *tramezzino* unique to Rome – half a sandwich on loaf bread containing tuna, chicken or egg salad, *prosciutto*, smoked salmon or other ingredients. Or try having sandwiches made at a local delicatessen *(alimentari)*. Ask for a *panino ripieno*, a bread roll filled with sausage, ham, cheese or salad.

Fast food and ethnic restaurants are becoming common sights. Chinese restaurants are popular, but you can also try African, Arab, Greek, Indian, Japanese, Lebanese and Mexican cuisines. Vegetarian restaurants are gaining in popularity.

In theory, the word *ristorante* usually indicates a larger and more elaborate establishment than a more cosy *trattoria* or rustic *osteria*. But in Rome the distinction is often blurred.

Price should not be taken as an indication of the quality of cuisine – an expensive restaurant may offer a superb meal with service to match, but often you pay for the location. Just a few streets off the famous tourist spots such as Piazza del Popolo and Piazza Navona, you'll find *trattorie* with lower prices, more appealing ambience and food with real character. Some restaurants offer fixed-price, three-course meals *(menù turistico* or

Cafés in Piazza della Rotonda

prezzo fisso) which will save money, but you almost always get better food by ordering individual dishes.

Roman restaurants serve lunch from 12.30 to 3pm and dinner from 8 to 11pm. Some offer late-night supper and are open until 1 or even 2am. Restaurants are usually closed one day a week, generally Sunday or Monday. It is better to book by telephone, especially for peak hours (around 1.30pm and 9pm) and peak days (Friday and Saturday).

What to Eat

Antipasti. Any *trattoria* worth its olive oil will have a display of its *antipasti* (hors d'oeuvre) on a table near the entrance. Make your choices and fill your plate. Both attractive and tasty are the cold *peperoni*: red, yellow and green peppers grilled, skinned and marinated in olive oil and garlic. Mushrooms *(funghi)*, artichokes *(carciofi)* and fennel *(finocchio)* come cold with an olive oil and salt-and-pepper dressing *(pinzimonio)*. A refreshing starter is *mozzarella alla caprese*, slices of soft *mozzarella* cheese and tomato with fresh basil and olive oil. Ham from Parma or San Daniele is paper thin, served with melon *(prosciutto con melone)* or figs *(con fichi)*.

Alfresco in Piazza del Popolo

Soups. Popular soups are vegetable *(minestrone)*, clear soup *(brodo)* and a light version with an egg beaten into it *(stracciatella)*.

Pasta. Traditionally served as an introductory course, not the main dish. Even the friendliest of restaurant owners will raise a sad eyebrow if you decide to make a meal out of a plate of spaghetti.

Besides spaghetti and macaroni try *tagliatelle* or the larger *fettuccine* ribbon noodles; baked *lasagne* with layers of pasta, meat sauce and béchamel; rolled *cannelloni*; and *ravioli*. From there, you launch into *tortellini* and *cappelletti* (variations on *ravioli*), or curved *linguine*, flat *pappardelle*, quill-shaped *penne* and corrugated *rigatoni*. There are almost as many sauces. The most famous, of course, is *bolognese*, or *ragù*. The tastiest version has not only minced beef, tomato and onions but chopped chicken livers, ham, carrots, celery, white wine and nutmeg. Other popular sauces are the simple *pomodoro* (tomato, garlic and basil), *aglio e olio* (garlic, olive oil and chilli), *carbonara* (chopped bacon and eggs), *matriciana* (pork cheek and tomato), *pesto* (basil and garlic ground in olive oil with pine nuts and Parmesan cheese) and *vongole* (clams).

Pizza. Another Italian invention familiar around the world, pizza is in reality a much more elaborate affair than you may be used to; the classic *margherita*, created in 1889 by a Neapolitan chef for Queen Margherita of Savoy, has tomato sauce and melted mozzarella. Toppings can include tomato, ham, anchovies, cheese, mushrooms, peppers, artichoke hearts, zucchini flowers, potatoes, egg, clams, tuna fish, garlic or any other ingredient that takes the cook's fancy. Note that in the summer pizzerias are not usually open for lunch because of the heat generated by their wood-fired ovens.

Meat. A normal steak served to one person in a US restaurant would feed a family of four in Italy. Portions are smaller, since Italians eat several courses. *Vitello* (veal) is very popular; Rome's speciality is *saltimbocca* (literally 'jump in the mouth'), a veal roll with ham, sage and Marsala wine. Try the *cotoletta* (pan-fried cutlet in breadcrumbs) or the *scaloppine al limone* (with lemon). *Ossobuco* is a delicious dish of stewed veal shin-bone in butter, with tomatoes, onions, finely chopped lemon rind and marrow.

Manzo (beef), *maiale* (pork) and *agnello* (lamb) are usually quite simple: charcoal-grilled or *al forno* (roasted). *Bistecca alla fiorentina* (grilled Florentine T-bone), the emperor of all steaks, costs a royal ransom, but you should try it once.

Romans also claim the best *capretto* (roast kid), *porchetta* (suckling pig, roasted whole on a spit) and *abbacchio* (spring lamb), flavoured with garlic, sage and rosemary and seasoned just before serving with anchovy paste. The most common chicken dishes are *pollo alla diavola* (grilled) or *petti di pollo alla bolognese* (filleted with ham and cheese).

Fish. This is prepared in a simple way – either grilled, steamed or fried. You should look out for *spigola* (sea bass), *rombo* (turbot), *triglia* (red mullet), *pesce spada* (swordfish), *orata* (gilthead), *sogliola* (sole) and *coda di rospo* (angler fish). The *fritto misto* is mixed seafood (fried), mostly shrimp and octopus.

Salami galore

Vegetables. These are ordered separately, as a *contorno* (side dish); they do not automatically come with the main course. What is available depends on the season, but usually includes *spinaci* (spinach), *cicoria* (chicory), *fagiolini* (string beans in butter and garlic), *piselli* (peas) and *zucchini* (courgettes).

Aristocrats among cooked vegetables are the *funghi porcini* (big boletus mushrooms), which are sometimes stuffed (*ripieni*) with bacon, garlic, parsley and cheese. The white truffle is an autumn delicacy and expensive. Try also *peperonata* (red peppers stewed with tomatoes) or *melanzane* (aubergine) sometimes stuffed with anchovies, olives and capers. The Jewish Ghetto originated *carciofi alla giudea* (fried whole artichokes).

Fresh market produce

Cheese. The famous *parmigiano* (Parmesan), far better than the exported product, is eaten separately, not just grated over soup or pasta. Try also the blue *gorgonzola*, creamy *fontina*, pungent cow's milk *taleggio,* or ewe's milk *pecorino*. *Ricotta* can be sweetened with sugar and cinnamon for a tasty dessert.

Dessert. This often means *gelato*, the creamiest ice cream in the world. It's usually better in an ice-cream parlour *(gelateria)* than in the average *trattoria*. *Zuppa inglese* (literally 'English soup'), the Italian version of trifle, can be anything from a thick and sumptuous mixture of fruit, cream, cake and Marsala to a disappointing sickly slice of cake. You may prefer the coffee-flavoured trifle or *tiramisù* (literally 'pick me up'). *Zabaglione* (whipped egg yolks, sugar and Marsala) should be served warm or sent back. *Panna cotta* (cooked cream with a fruit or chocolate topping) and crème caramel (an egg custard flan) are also popular staples. Fresh fruit can be a succulent alternative: *fragole* (strawberries), served with whipped cream or lemon, *ananas* (pineapple) and in summer a cool slice of *anguria* (watermelon).

Drinks

Wine. Most restaurants offer the open wine of the house, red or white, in 1/4-litre, 1/2-litre or 1-litre carafes, as well as a good selection of bottled vintages. Rome's 'local' wine comes from the surrounding province of Lazio. The whites from the Alban Hills, called Castelli Romani, are light and pleasant and can be sweet or dry. The most famous is Frascati. From further afield, the Chiantis of Tuscany are available everywhere, as are the velvety Valpolicella from the Veneto and Piedmont's full-bodied Barolo. Look out for the unusual Est! Est! Est! from Montefiascone on Lake Bolsena.

Italian beer. Beer is tasty but not as strong as north European brands. Nastro Azzuro is a national favourite.

Have an *aperitivo* before dinner

Aperitivo. Campari with soda and lemon is drunk as a refreshing appetiser, as is fizzy white Prosecco wine from the Veneto region. For after-dinner drinks, try a glass of aniseed-flavoured *sambuca* with a *mosca* (coffee bean, literally a fly) swimming in it. Other alternatives are *grappa*, distilled from grapes, or icy *limoncello*, a liqueur made from lemons.

To Help You Order…

Waiters are called **cameriere** (men) or **cameriera** (women).

Do you have a set menu? **Avete un menù a prezzo fisso?**

I'd like a/an/some… **Vorrei…**

beer	**una birra**	pepper	**del pepe**
bread	**del pane**	potatoes	**delle patate**
butter	**del burro**	salad	**un'insalata**
coffee	**un caffè**	salt	**del sale**
fish	**del pesce**	soup	**una minestra**
fruit	**della frutta**	sugar	**dello zucchero**
ice cream	**un gelato**	tea	**un tè**
meat	**della carne**	water	**dell'acqua**
milk	**del latte**	wine	**del vino**

…and Read the Menu

aglio	garlic	**manzo**	beef
agnello	lamb	**mela**	apple
albicocche	apricots	**melanzane**	aubergine
aragosta	lobster	**merluzzo**	cod
arancia	orange	**ostriche**	oysters
bistecca	beefsteak	**pesca**	peach
braciola	chop	**piselli**	peas
calamari	squid	**pollo**	chicken
carciofi	artichokes	**pomodori**	tomatoes
cipolle	onions	**prosciutto**	ham
crostacei	shellfish	**rognoni**	kidneys
fegato	liver	**tacchino**	turkey
fichi	figs	**tonno**	tuna
formaggio	cheese	**uovo**	egg
frutti di mare	seafood	**uva**	grapes
funghi	mushrooms	**verdure**	vegetables
lamponi	raspberries	**vitello**	veal
maiale	pork	**vongole**	clams

HANDY TRAVEL TIPS

An A–Z Summary of Practical Information

A

ACCOMMODATION (See also CAMPING, YOUTH HOSTELS and the list of RECOMMENDED HOTELS starting on page 128)

Rome's array of lodgings ranges from the spartan to the palatial. Hotels *(alberghi)* are classified in five categories, graded from one to five stars, based on the amenities and comfort they offer. (The Italian Tourist Board no longer uses the term *pensione* in its classifications; these family-style boarding houses are now graded as hotels, usually one or two stars.) Some religious institutions also take guests at reasonable rates.

High season is considered to be Christmas, New Year and Easter to October (though many avoid the hot and humid months of July and August). At these times booking ahead is important. For the rest of the year you can normally find accommodation in your preferred category without difficulty, although decent inexpensive hotels are usually booked far ahead. The Rome Tourist Board (APT) has up-to-date hotel information (see TOURIST INFORMATION). The APT has information offices at the (Roma-Nord) Salaria service area on the A1 *autostrada* (motorway) and at the (Roma-Sud) Frascati service area on the A2 *autostrada*. Alternatively, H.R. Hotel Reservation offers a free reservation service (tel: 06-97745496, <www.hotelreservation.it>) and has desks at Fiumicino airport and Termini railway station.

Room rates should include taxes and service. Most hotels now have air-conditioning; in lower category hotels it sometimes costs extra.

Termini station has luggage storage facilities for those with hours to kill between trains. At Fiumicino, the Hilton Rome Airport is near the main terminal (tel: 06-65258, fax: 06-65256525).

I'd like a single/double room with bath/shower.	**Vorrei una camera singola/ doppia con bagno/doccia**
What's the rate per night?	**Qual è il prezzo per notte?**

AIRPORTS (Aeroporti)

Rome is served by two airports, Leonardo da Vinci, more commonly referred to as **Fiumicino**, 30km (18 miles) southwest of the city, and **Ciampino**, 15km (9 miles) southeast of the city on the Via Appia Nuova. Fiumicino handles mainly scheduled air traffic; Ciampino is used by most charter companies and low-cost airlines.

Fiumicino is connected by train to Termini railway station (about every half hour; journey 30 minutes; first and last departures 6.35am and 11.35pm), and to Trastevere railway station (every 15 minutes, after 9.27pm every 30 minutes; journey 23 minutes; first and last departures 5.57am and 11.27pm). A late night COTRAL bus runs between Fiumicino and the Tiburtina and Termini train stations when there is no train service. Termini is connected to metro lines A and B, and to buses that go all over the city; Trastevere is linked to the city centre by tram No. 8. There's also the Terravision coach service between Termini train station and Fiumicino and Ciampino airports. Buy tickets online, <www.terravision.it>, at the airports' Terravision kiosk or at Termini station's Via Marsala entrance (agenzia 365).

Information: Fiumicino, tel: 06-65951; Ciampino, tel: 06-794941; Rome airports website: <www.adr.it>; national train timetables and phone bookings, tel: 892021, <www.trenitalia.com>.

B

BUDGETING FOR YOUR TRIP

Airport transfer. Train from Fiumicino Airport to Roma Termini €11; to Trastevere railway station €5. Bus from Ciampino Airport to Anagnina Metro station €1. (You will need to get a different ticket, also costing €1, for the metro from Anagnina to Rome's central station Termini.) Taxi from Fiumicino to city centre, minimum €40–45. **Buses, metro and trains (urban network).** Standard fare (biglietto) €1 (valid for 75 minutes); day ticket (BIG or biglietto integrato giornaliero) €4; weekly ticket (CIS or carta integrata settimanale)

€16; tourists' ticket (BTI or *biglietto turistico integrato*) €11, which allows unlimited travel on all trams, local trains, COTRAL buses and the metro for three full days.

Car hire. Prices per day at all the major international firms start at about €60 for the smallest cars. Expect to pay a surcharge for unlimited mileage. Italy Rent (<www.italyrent.it>) has cheaper prices and also has an office at the airport.

Entertainment. Cinema €7.50, nightclub (entry and first drink) €15–25, outdoor opera €20–50.

Hotels (double room with bath, including tax and service). Prices range from €45 for a one-star hotel (cheaper if it has dorm-beds) near the station to over €1,200 for a suite in a five-star near the Spanish Steps. Almost all hotels lower their prices in the low season so it is worth haggling if you think you're being taken advantage of.

Meals and drinks. Continental breakfast €8, lunch/dinner in a fairly good establishment €20–50, coffee served at a table €2.50–5, served at the bar €0.65–1.20. Also at the bar: bottle of beer €1.60–2.50, soft drinks €1.50–3, aperitif €3 and up.

Museums. €4–10.

Taxis. The meter starts at €2.33 (€4.91 10pm–7am), and €0.78 is charged for each kilometre in town (€1.29 outside town). There is a surcharge for holidays, Sundays and luggage (each piece costs €1.04).

C

CAMPING (*campeggio*)

Rome and the surrounding countryside have some 20 official camp-sites, most equipped with electricity, water, and toilet facilities. They are listed in the telephone directory under *Campeggi, ostelli e villaggi turistici*. You can also ask in any tourist information point (*see page 126*) for a comprehensive list of sites and rates. Rates are usually around €8–10 per person per night; caravan (trailer) €9; camper €9; tent €8; car €5; motorbike €3.50. Prices go down in low season.

> Is there a campsite near here?   **C'è un campeggio qui vicino?**
> We have a tent/caravan (trailer).   **Abbiamo la tenda/la roulotte.**

The Touring Club Italiano (TCI) and the Automobile Club d'Italia (ACI) also publish lists of campsites and tourist villages, available at bookstores or the Tourist Office. You are strongly advised to stick to the official campsites. If you enter Italy with a caravan (trailer), you are expected to show an inventory (with two copies) of all the material and equipment in the caravan, such as dishes and linen.

CAR HIRE *(Autonoleggio; see also* DRIVING*)*

The major firms, Hertz, Avis, Budget and Maggiore, have offices at the airports as well as in the city. To hire a car you must be at least 21 years of age and have held a valid driving licence for at least a year. Mandatory third-party insurance is included in the rates. A car hired in one Italian city can be dropped off in another, usually for an added cost. Hiring a car is expensive in Italy (see BUDGETING FOR YOUR TRIP), and it is almost always cheaper and more convenient to book in advance from home, or as part of a fly-drive package. Before you leave home, review what is covered and what is not with your home-based office, and check the coverage offered by your credit card.

> I would like to rent a car   **Vorrei noleggiare una macchina**
>   for one day   **per un giorno**
>   for one week   **per una settimana**

CLIMATE

From June to mid-September, temperatures in Rome range from warm to very hot. It is not unusual to find temperatures above 32°C (90°F) in the afternoon in July and August, when it is best to do major sightseeing in the morning and late afternoon.

Winters are cool, often cold, and at times rainy, with occasional snow, but there are many sunny days. Spring and autumn are mild, and the best time to visit.

	J	F	M	A	M	J	J	A	S	O	N	D
Max °F	52	55	59	66	74	82	87	86	79	71	61	55
°C	11	13	15	19	23	28	31	30	26	22	16	13
Min °F	40	42	45	50	56	63	67	67	62	55	49	44
°C	4	5	7	10	12	17	19	19	18	13	9	6

COMPLAINTS *(Reclami)*

Complaints should first be made to the management *(direttore)* of the establishment concerned. If satisfaction is not obtained, threaten to make a formal declaration *(faccio la denuncia alla questura)* although carrying this out will consume many precious days of your visit. To avoid problems, always establish a price in advance with all parties involved, such as porters at stations. For taxi fare complaints, refer to a notice, in four languages, which is affixed by law in each taxi, specifying extra charges (for airport runs, baggage surcharge, Sunday or holiday rates, night surcharge, etc).

CONSULATES *(Consolati)*

Contact the offices of your diplomatic representative if you lose your passport or run into serious trouble. Consulates can also provide lists of English-speaking doctors, lawyers and interpreters.

Australia: Via Antonio Bosio 5, tel: 06-852721.
Canada: Via Zara 30, tel: 06-854441.
Ireland: Piazza Campitelli 3, tel: 06-6979121.
New Zealand: Via Zara 28, tel: 06-4417171.
South Africa: Via Tanaro 14, tel: 06-852541.
UK: Via XX Settembre 80a, tel: 06-42200001.
US: Via Vittorio Veneto 121, tel: 06-46741.

CRIME AND SAFETY (see also EMERGENCIES)

Pickpockets and purse-snatchers are not uncommon in Rome, and tourists are a favourite target. Carry with you only what is absolutely necessary; leave passports, airline tickets and all but one credit card in the hotel safe. Use a money belt or carry valuables in an inside pocket. For women, a small purse worn bandolier-style or under a coat in winter is best. Be careful on crowded public transport (beware the tourist-filled buses 64 and 40 from Termini station to the Vatican, and the metro). Groups of begging children holding signs and trying to distract you, are adept pickpockets, lingering around Termini, the Forum, Largo di Torre Argentina and crowded shopping streets.

Never leave anything in a parked car. Always lock it, with the glove compartment open, to discourage prospective thieves. When possible, park in a garage or attended parking area.

Make photocopies of your airline tickets, driving licence, passport, and other vital documents to facilitate reporting any theft and obtaining replacements. Report thefts to the police, so that you have a statement to file with your insurance claim. The central police station is at Questura Centrale, Via San Vitale 15, tel: 06-46861.

I want to report a theft.	**Voglio denunciare un furto.**
My wallet/handbag/passport/	**Mi hanno rubato**
ticket has been stolen.	**il portafoglio/la borsa/**
	il passaporto/il biglietto.

CUSTOMS AND ENTRY REQUIREMENTS

For citizens of EU countries, a valid passport or identity card is all that is needed to enter Italy for up to 90 days. Citizens of Australia, Canada, New Zealand and the US require only a valid passport.

Visas (*permesso di soggiorno*). For stays of more than 90 days a visa or residence permit is required. Regulations change from time to time, so check with the Italian Embassy in your home country first.

| I have nothing to declare. | **Non ho nulla da dichiarare.** |
| It's for my personal use. | **È per mio uso personale.** |

Customs. Free exchange of non-duty-free goods for personal use is allowed between EU countries. Refer to your home country's regulating organisation for a current complete list of import restrictions.

Currency restrictions. Tourists may bring an unlimited amount of Italian or foreign currency into the country. On departure you must declare any currency beyond the equivalent of €10,000, so it's wise to declare sums exceeding this amount when you arrive.

D

DISABLED VISITORS

Cobbled streets and steep hills are just two of the problems facing travellers with disabilities in Rome. There are lavatories for disabled people at both the airports, at Stazione Termini and Piazza San Pietro. St Peter's, the Vatican Museums, Castel Sant'Angelo, Galleria Doria Pamphili, San Giovanni in Laterano, Galleria Borghese, Galleria Nazionale d'Arte Moderno and a few minor museums are wheelchair accessible. Up-to-date information on access to sights, monuments and hotels is available from Roma Per Tutti (Mon–Fri 9am–5pm, tel: 06-57177094, also English speaking; <www.romapertutti.it>).

DRIVING

Entering Italy. To bring your car into Italy, you will need:
- an international driving licence or valid national one
- car registration papers
- green insurance card (an extension to your ordinary insurance, making your policy valid for Italy)
- a red warning triangle in case of breakdown
- national identity sticker for your car.

patente	driving licence
libretto di circolazione	car registration papers
carta verde	green card

Drivers of cars that are not their own must have the owner's written permission. Before leaving home, check with your motoring association about the latest status of petrol coupons (these give tourists access to cheaper fuel) in Italy, as their availability is constantly changing.

Rules and regulations. Seat belts are compulsory in Italy. Drive on the right, overtake on the left. Traffic on major roads has right of way over that entering from side roads, but this is frequently ignored, so be very careful. At intersections of roads of similar importance, the car on the right theoretically has the right of way. When passing other vehicles, or remaining in the left-hand (overtaking) lane, keep your directional indicator flashing. Since autumn 2002, it has also been compulsory to keep your headlights on when out of the city, in other words on all *autostrade* (motorways) and the so-called *strade statali* (state roads). The car must also contain one high-visibility fluorescent jacket to be worn if the car breaks down.

The speed limit on the *autostrade* is 130km/h (80mph); on other roads the limit is 90km/h (55mph). The limit in built-up areas is generally 60km/h (37mph). The traffic police *(polizia stradale)* patrol the highways and byways on motorcycles or in Alfa Romeos, usually light blue. Speeding fines often have to be paid on the spot – ask for a receipt *(ricevuta)*.

All cities and many towns and villages have signs posted on the outskirts with the phone number of the local traffic police or *carabinieri*. The Rome headquarters are at Viale Romania 45, tel: 06-80981.

Are we on the right road for...?	**Siamo sulla strada giusta per...?**

Driving in Rome. Only the most intrepid motorist stays cool in the face of the Romans' hair-raising driving habits. However, Roman drivers are not reckless – simply attuned to a different concept of driving. If you observe the following ground rules and venture with prudence into the urban traffic whirlpool, you stand a good chance of coming out unscathed.

Check to the right and left and your rearview mirror all the time; don't take priority for granted with green lights and pedestrian crossings. To progress in a traffic jam, inch gently but confidently forward into the snarl-up. Being too polite is tantamount to abdicating your rights as a motorist. Be careful of *motorini* (scooters) suddenly passing you on either side.

In the city centre between the river, Piazza del Popolo, Piazza di Spagna, Santa Maria Maggiore and the Colosseum, as well as in the San Lorenzo district and across the river in Trastevere, a traffic-restricted *zona a traffico limitato (ZTL)* operates Mon–Thur 6.30am– 6pm, Fri 6.30am–6pm and 11pm–3am, and Sat 2pm–6pm and 11pm– 3am. Exceptions to this rule are taxis, buses and cars with permits.

If you need help. Emergency telephone boxes are located at regular intervals on the *autostrade* in case of breakdowns or other difficulties. The ACI (Automobile Club of Italy) runs an efficient breakdown service. If you dial **803116** you can access their English-speaking operators 24 hours a day. ACI temporary membership can be arranged at main border crossings.

I've had a breakdown.	**Ho avuto un guasto.**
There's been an accident.	**C'è stato un incidente.**

Fuel. Service stations abound in Italy, usually with at least one mechanic on duty. Most stations close all day on Sundays, and on other days of the week at 7.30pm (some close earlier, and some close for an hour or two at lunchtime). However, many service stations have self-service pumps, which are available during closing hours and accept pristine banknotes. Stations along the *autostrade* are open 24 hours a day. Fuel *(benzina)* comes unleaded *(senza piombo* or *verde)* or as diesel *(gasolio)*. Liquid propane gas is marked GPL.

Fill the tank, please.	**Per favore, faccia il pieno.**
Super/normal	**super/normale**
Unleaded	**senza piombo/verde**
Diesel	**gasolio**
Check the oil/tyres/battery.	**Controlli l'olio/i pneumatici/ la batteria.**

Parking. Parking is one of Rome's greatest challenges. Your wisest course is to find an affordable car park for the duration of your stay and walk or use public transport. Paid parking areas are designated by blue lines. Buy a ticket from one of the coin-accepting meters: €1 per hour, available in increments of 15 minutes. Leave the meter-issued ticket, on which the time of purchase is printed, inside the windscreen (if you overstay your time, you'll be ticketed).

If you park in a tow-away zone, you will pay a heavy fine and spend precious time reclaiming your car. For towed away or clamped cars, contact the *vigili urbani* (municipal police) central headquarters at Via della Consolazione 1, tel: 06-67691. In the centre of Rome the largest and most accessible car parks are: Terminal Gianicolo at Piazza Rovere, tel: 06-6840331, open 6am–1.30am; Parking Ludovisi at Via Ludovisi 60, tel: 06-4740632, open 5.30am–1.30am; or (the largest, always open) at Villa Borghese, entrance at Viale del Galoppatoio 33, tel: 06-3225934.

Where's the nearest car park?	**Dov'è il parcheggio più vicino?**
Can I park here?	**Posso parcheggiare qui?**

Road signs. Most road signs employed in Italy are international pictographs, but below are some written ones you may come across.

Accendere le luci	Use headlights
Curva pericolosa	Dangerous bend/curve
Deviazione	Detour
Divieto di sorpasso	No overtaking
Divieto di sosta	No stopping/parking
Lavori in corso	Road works
Passaggio a livello	Level crossing
Pericolo	Danger
Rallentare	Slow down
Senso unico	One-way street
Senso vietato/Vietato l'ingresso	No entry
Zona pedonale	Pedestrian zone

E

ELECTRICITY

Electric current is 220 volts, 50 Hz AC. Bring a multiple adapter plug *(un adattatore)*, or buy one as required.

EMERGENCIES

In an emergency you can phone the following numbers all over Italy 24 hours a day: General Emergency Number (for all services) **113**; *Carabinieri* (emergency services) **112**; Ambulance **118**; Fire **115**; Road assistance (ACI) **803116**.

Careful!	**Attenzione!**
Help!	**Aiuto!**
Stop thief!	**Al ladro!**

G

GETTING THERE (see also AIRPORTS)

A reliable travel agent will have full details of all the latest flight possibilities, fares and regulations, or do your own search on the internet (see WEBSITES).

By air. Rome's Fiumicino (Leonardo da Vinci) Airport is linked by frequent direct service to cities in Europe, North America, the Middle East and Africa. Average flying times are: New York–Rome 8 hours; Los Angeles–Rome 13 hours; London–Rome 2 hours 30 minutes; Sydney–Rome 26 hours.

By car. The Channel Tunnel and Cross-Channel car ferries link the UK with France, Belgium, and Holland. Once on the Continent, you can put your car on a train to Milan (starting points include Boulogne, Paris and Cologne). Alternatively, you can drive from the Channel coast to Rome without leaving a motorway. The main north–south (Milan–Florence–Reggio di Calabria) and east–west (L'Aquila–Civitavecchia) motorways connect with Rome via a huge ring motorway (grande raccordo anulare).

By rail. InterRail cards are valid in Italy, as is the **Eurailpass** for non-European residents (purchase it before you leave home). You can find out more details at the Rail Europe Travel Centre at 178 Piccadilly, London, W1J 9A (tel: 0870 8371 371; <www.raileurope.co.uk>).

GUIDES AND TOURS

Most hotels in Rome can arrange for multilingual guides or interpreters. At many museums and sites, audio tour commentaries can be rented. The Italian Tourist Agency (**CIT**, Via Barberini 27, tel: 06-42014238; <www.citviaggi.it>), and many private firms offer guided bus tours of all the major sites, plus excursions to other points of interest. Often tourists are picked up and dropped off at their hotels. A private all-purpose English-speaking travel operation located near the station, **Enjoy Rome** (Via Marghera 8a, tel: 06-4451843, <www.enjoyrome.com>), offers inexpensive walking tours of Rome daily.

Rome's municipal bus company, **ATAC**, provides a sightseeing tour which takes in many of the major sites. The open-topped double-decker bus **110 Open** leaves every 20 minutes from in front of Termini station (daily from 8.40am–8.20pm) and tours the city's main monuments. Tickets cost €13 and can be bought at the terminus (or on board if you are getting on at one of the stops en route). The whole tour of 11 stops lasts two hours but you can get on and off all day.

Archeobus is an environmentally-friendly minibus service that departs hourly from Piazza dei Cinquecento (in front of Termini) between 9.45am and 4.45pm bound for the beautiful Appia Antica Park, making 15 stops at historic sites and monuments. Ticket cost €8. A joint ticket for the 110 Open and Archeobus can be purchased for €20. For details of both services, tel: 06-46952252, <www.trambus.com>.

Three electric minibuses (tickets €1) travel through the historic centre all day: the 116 passes through or near Campo de' Fiori, Piazza Farnese, Piazza Navona, the Pantheon and Piazza Barberini; the 119 serves the area around Piazza del Popolo and Piazza di Spagna; the 117 goes from Piazza del Popolo to Basilica San Giovanni in Laterano.

H

HEALTH AND MEDICAL CARE

EU residents should obtain the European Health Insurance Card, available in the UK from post offices or online <www.ehic.org.uk>, entitling them to emergency medical and hospital treatment. To cover all eventualities, travel insurance is recommended. Non-EU visitors should always have private medical insurance. If your private health insurance policy does not cover you while abroad, take out a short-term policy.

Ask your hotel receptionist if you need a doctor (or dentist) who speaks English. The US and British consulates (see CONSULATES) have lists of English-speaking doctors. Local Health Units of the Italian National Health Service are listed in the telephone directory under *Azienda Sanitaria Locale (ASL)*. The first-aid (*pronto soccorso*, or 'Emergency Room') section of hospitals handles medical emergencies.

Pharmacies. The Italian *farmacia* is open during shopping hours (see OPENING HOURS). Usually one operates out of hours in each district on a rotating basis. Some are open 24 hours, like the Farmacia della Stazione in Piazza dei Cinquecento 49–51, on the corner with Via Cavour (tel: 06-4880019).

I need a doctor/a dentist.	**Ho bisogno di un medico/dentista.**
Where's the nearest (all-night) chemist?	**Dov'è la farmacia (di turno) più vicina?**

HOLIDAYS *(Festa)*

Banks, government offices and most shops and museums close on public holidays. When a major holiday falls on a Thursday or a Tuesday, Italians may make a *ponte* (bridge) to the weekend, meaning that Friday or Monday is taken, too. The most important holidays are:

1 January	*Capodanno*	New Year's Day
6 January	*Epifania*	Epiphany
25 April	*Festa della Liberazione*	Liberation Day
1 May	*Primo Maggio*	May Day
15 August	*Ferragosto*	Feast of the Assumption
1 November	*Ognissanti*	All Saints' Day
8 December	*Immacolata Concezione*	Immaculate Conception
25 December	*Natale*	Christmas Day
26 December	*Santo Stefano*	Boxing Day
Moveable date:	*Pasquetta*	Easter Monday

In addition, Rome has a local holiday on 29 June, the *Festa di San Pietro e San Paolo*, the Feast of St Peter and St Paul, the city's patron saints, when many offices and shops close. Get to St Peter's Square early, as there are huge crowds.

L

LANGUAGE

You will not find English spoken everywhere in Rome, as you do in some other European cities. However, Italians are usually helpful and quick to understand what you want. Italians appreciate foreigners making an effort to speak their language, even if it's only a few words. In the major hotels and shops, staff usually speak some English.

Bear in mind the following tips on pronunciation:

'**c**' is pronounced like 'ch' in change when followed by 'e' or 'i'.

'**ch**' together sounds like the 'c' in cat.

'**g**' followed by an 'e' or an 'i' is pronounced like 'j' in jet.

'**gh**' together sounds like the 'g' in gap.

'**gl**' together sounds like the 'lli' in million.

'**gn**' is pronounced like 'ni' in onion.

'**sc**'+ 'i' is pronounced like 'she'.

M

MAPS *(Piante)*

The offices of the Rome Tourist Board give away basic street plans featuring a selection of local information including the whereabouts and opening hours of all the principal monuments and museums. More detailed maps are on sale at newsstands. A free bus, tram and metro network map is available at the ATAC offices at Via Volturno 59 (across from Termini station, mornings and weekdays only) or from ticket booths at the Ottaviano and Spagna metro stops on line A. Even more comprehensive public transport maps can be bought from any newsagent and <www.atac.roma.it> offers a useful journey planner.

MEDIA

A wide selection of English-language newspapers and magazines are on sale at the airport and main railway station, and at newsstands in the centre. The supplement *Trovaroma*, published in the Thursday edition of the newspaper *La Repubblica*, provides listings of cultural events in Rome. Other publications are the weekly English section of *Roma C'è* (out Wednesdays) and the monthly magazine WHERE Rome, which lists events and shopping and eating possibilities, and is available in many hotels. Another useful English-language publication is the fortnightly *Wanted in Rome* (<www.wantedinrome.com>).

The RAI, Italy's state broadcasting system, has three TV channels. There are also various private national and local channels. LA7 offers Fox News broadcasts during the early morning hours (and many hotels offer CNN around the clock). Vatican Radio carries foreign-language religious news programmes. British (BBC), American (VOA) and Canadian (CBC) stations are easily obtained on most radios.

Have you any English-language newspapers?	**Avete quotidiani in inglese?**

MONEY

Currency. Italy's monetary unit is the euro (abbreviated €), which is divided into 100 cents. Banknotes are available in denominations of 500, 200, 100, 50, 20, 10 and 5 euros. There are coins for 2 and 1 euro, and for 50, 20, 10, 5, 2 and 1 cent.

Currency exchange. Currency exchange offices *(cambio)* in the touristy areas are usually open daily 8.30am–7.30pm; some may close on Sunday. Both *cambio* and banks charge a commission. Banks generally offer higher exchange rates and lower commissions. Passports are sometimes required when changing money.

ATMs. Automatic currency-exchange machines are operated by many banks, and all banks have ATMs *(bancomat)* that work with cashpoint cards featuring any of the major credit card symbols. Check with your bank at home to make sure your PIN number is valid in Italy.

Credit cards and travellers' cheques. Most hotels, shops and restaurants take credit cards. If the card's sign is posted in the window they must accept it, although some will try to avoid doing so. Travellers' cheques are not accepted everywhere; it is advisable to exchange them at a bank (where you will get better value) at the start of your stay. Passports are required when cashing travellers' cheques.

I want to change some pounds/dollars.	**Desidero cambiare delle sterline/dei dollari.**
Do you accept travellers' cheques?	**Accetta i travellers cheques?**
Can I pay with a credit card?	**Posso pagare con la carta di credito?**

OPENING HOURS

Many offices, larger stores and tourist-orientated shops operate nonstop all day. But much of the city shuts or slows down after lunch.

Shops. Mon–Sat 9am–1pm and 4–8pm (winter 3.30–7.30pm). Half-day closing is usually Monday morning. However, most shops in the centre (Via del Corso, Via Nazionale, Via del Tritone) are open 10am–7pm, and department stores are also open all day. Food stores are open 8.30am–1.30pm and 4–7.30pm (summer until 8pm). Except for supermarkets, there is a half-day closing, usually Thursday afternoon in winter, and Saturday afternoon in summer. Most shops in the city centre or in commercial districts, including supermarkets, now stay open through lunch and on Sunday. Expect many of the smaller shops and boutiques to be closed for at least two weeks between July and mid-September.

Post offices. Mon–Fri 8.30am–2pm, until 1pm Sat. The main post office, Piazza San Silvestro, is open Mon–Sat 8am–7pm. The post office at the station (on Via Giolitti) is open Mon–Fri 8am–7pm, Sat 8am–1.15pm.

Banks. Mon–Fri 8.30am–1.30pm, and again for two hours or so in the afternoon (usually 2.40–4.30pm). A few banks are also open on Saturday mornings.

Pharmacies. 8.30am–1pm and 4–8pm (some 24 hrs, *see page 116*).

Churches. Open daily from early morning to noon or 12.30pm, and 4 or 5–7pm. They discourage Sunday morning visits except for those attending Mass. Larger churches and basilicas are open all day.

Museums and historic sites. These are usually open Tues–Sun, 9am–7pm (sometimes earlier). These hours vary, so check with your hotel or the tourist office before setting off.

P

POLICE

The municipal police *(vigili urbani)*, dressed in navy blue or summer white uniforms with white helmets, handle city traffic and other city police tasks. They are courteous and helpful to tourists, though they rarely speak a foreign language. Interpreters display a special badge, which indicates the languages they speak.

The *carabinieri*, in dark blue uniforms with a red stripe down their trousers, deal with theft, serious crimes, demonstrations and military affairs. The national, or state, police *(polizia di stato)*, distinguished by their navy-blue jackets and light-blue trousers, handle other police and administrative matters. (See also DRIVING.) The all-purpose emergency number, **113**, will get you police assistance.

| Where's the nearest police station? | Dov'è il posto di polizia più vicino? |

POST OFFICES *(posta or ufficio postale)*

Post offices handle telegrams, mail and money transfers. Look for the yellow sign with PT in blue. Postage stamps are also sold at tobacconists and at some hotel desks. Post boxes are mostly red – the slot marked *Per la Città* is for local mail only, the one labelled *Altre Destinazioni* is for all other destinations; blue post boxes are for international mail only. For more efficient delivery ask for *posta prioritaria* stamps. This way you are guaranteed delivery within three days in Europe and between five and nine days elsewhere in the world.

There is a *poste restante* service (also called *fermo posta)* at the main post office in Piazza San Silvestro. Don't forget your passport for identification when you go to pick up mail. A small fee is payable.

Telegrams *(telegrammi)* and telex messages can be sent to destinations inside and outside Italy. Fax service is available, here or through most hotels.

I'd like a stamp for this letter/ postcard.	**Desidero un francobollo per questa lettera/cartolina.**

PUBLIC TRANSPORT

Metropolitana (underground/subway). Rome has two underground railway lines, designated Line A and Line B. Line A runs from Battistini in the west of the city southeast to Anagnina, stopping at more than 20 stations and passing close to many of Rome's popular tourist sights (including the Vatican Museums and the Spanish Steps). The intersecting Line B runs from Rebibbia in the northeastern part of the city through Stazione Termini to Laurentina (passing by the Colosseum and the suburb of EUR) in the southwest. The two lines intersect only once, at Stazione Termini. Local trains to Ostia Antica and Lido di Ostia (Rome's closest beach) leave from the train station adjacent to the Piramide metro stop (Line B). The metro runs 5.30am–11.30pm (Sat until 12.30am). Note that Line

A currently closes at 9pm for engineering works (until 2008). From 9–11.30pm (Sat until 12.30am), a replacement bus service (MA1 and MA2) follows the same route.

Metro stations are identified by a large red sign containing a white letter 'M'. Tickets are sold at newsstands and tobacconists, but can also be purchased from machines at the metro stations.

Buses *(autobus)*. Rome's red, green and orange buses serve every corner of the city. Although crowded on certain routes and at rush hours, they are an inexpensive way of getting around. Each bus stop *(fermata)* indicates the buses stopping there, their routes, and frequency. Buses run 5.30pm–midnight, after which there is a night service. Tickets for buses must be bought in advance from ATAC booths, some newsstands and tobacconists, or automatic dispensers. Enter the bus by the rear or front doors and punch your ticket in a machine; exit by the middle doors; remember that you must ring before your stop.

A single ticket is valid for 75 minutes and can be used on as many buses as you wish, but can be used only once on the metro or train. 24-hour tickets (BIG) let you travel as much as you like by train, bus and metro. Weekly tickets (CIS) are sold at the ATAC (transport authority) information booth in Piazza dei Cinquecento, in front of Stazione Termini. Detailed network maps can be purchased from newsstands. For detailed information on public transport contact ATAC, tel: 800-431784 (freephone), <www.atac.roma.it>.

Where's the nearest bus stop/ underground (subway) station?	**Dov'è la fermata d'autobus/ la stazione della metropolitana più vicina?**
When's the next bus/train to…?	**Quando parte il prossimo autobus/treno per…?**
I'd like a ticket to…	**Vorrei un biglietto per…**
single (one-way)	**andata**
return (round trip)	**andata e ritorno**

COTRAL (<www.cotralspa.it>) operates bus services to the outskirts of Rome. Buses to the Roman hills (Albano, Frascati, Castel Gandolfo and so on) leave from the Anagnina metro station.

Horse-drawn carriages (*carrozzelle*). A familiar sight in Rome for centuries, carriages now number only a few dozen. They can be found at many of the major tourist sites, including the Pantheon, St Peter's Square, the Spanish Steps and the Colosseum. A complete tour around the centre of the city starts at €80.

Taxis (*tassì or taxi*). Rome's licensed white taxis can be flagged, but it is easier to find them at taxi ranks, which are in various strategic points of the city (in the historic centre two useful ones are located at Largo di Torre Argentina and Piazza Venezia, on the western side of Piazza Madonna di Loreto), or summon them by telephone (tel: 06-6645 or 06-3570). When you phone for a taxi, you will have to pay a surcharge. Extra fees are also charged for luggage, public holidays, Sundays, airport trips and after 10pm: by law, the rates are posted in four languages inside all taxis. Tariffs outside the GRA (Rome's major ring road) are much higher. Tips are optional but much appreciated. Beware of the non-metered unlicensed taxis (*abusivi*), which charge much more than the normal taxi rates. They are often found at the airport and railway stations.

R

RELIGION

Roman Catholic Mass is celebrated every day and several times on Sunday in Italian. A few Catholic churches have occasional services in English. Confessions are heard in English in St Peter's, Santa Maria Maggiore, San Giovanni in Laterano and San Paolo Fuori le Mura.

A number of non-Catholic denominations have services in English. These include the Church of England at All Saints, Via del Babuino 153B; Anglican Episcopal at St Paul's, Via Napoli 58; Scottish Presbyterian at St Andrew's, Via XX Settembre 7; Methodist at

Piazza Ponte Sant'Angelo. The Jewish Synagogue is at Lungotevere Cenci 9. The city's mosque is in Via della Moschea.

T

TELEPHONES *(Telefono)*

Public phone booths are scattered at strategic locations throughout the city. Calls can also be made from bars and cafés, indicated by a yellow telephone sign showing a telephone dial and receiver. Public pay phones require phone cards *(scheda telefonica)* that cost from €2.50 upwards. To make a call from a pay phone, insert the card (with the serrated corner torn off) and lift the receiver.

Since Telecom Italia operates one of the most expensive phone services in Europe it may be a good idea to buy an international phone card while staying in Rome. Sold at most newsagents these cards allow you to call abroad at very low cost using a freephone number. Two of the best ones for the UK and US are called Europa and Eurocity, which come in €5 or €10 versions.

International calls from hotels are heavily surcharged; it is advisable that you use an American calling card for overseas calls. To connect with local service when using a calling card, dial 800-172444 for AT&T, and for MCI Worldphone dial 800-905825.

For Italian directory enquiries, **1254**; international enquiries, **892 412**, national and international calls via 24-hour operator, **170**; Yellow Pages enquiries, **1240**; direct dialling for Australia, 0061; Canada, 001; Ireland, 00353; South Africa, 0027; UK, 0044; US, 001.

Give me … coins/phone card please.	**Per favore, mi dia … monete/ una scheda telefonica.**
€5/€25	**cinque/venticinque euro**
Can you get me this number in…?	**Può passarmi questo numero in…?**

TIME ZONES

Italy follows Central European Time (GMT + 1). From the last Sunday in March to the last Sunday in September, clocks are put ahead one hour (GMT + 2). The following is a chart of summer times:

New York	London	Italy	Jo'burg	Sydney	Auckland
6am	11am	**noon**	noon	8pm	10pm

TIPPING

Though a service charge (either called *servizio* or *coperto, coperti* plural, which is basically a small cover charge per person) is added to most restaurant bills, it is customary to leave an additional nominal tip of a few euros. Leave up to €5 depending on the size of the bill. It is also usual to give porters, doormen, garage attendants and others a little something for their services.

Italians do not generally tip very generously, which means that anything you give as a tourist will be very much appreciated and probably far more than a Roman would give. As a rough guide, give a hotel porter €1.50 per bag; a chambermaid €3 per day; a lavatory attendant €0.50. Tip hairdressers and tour guides up to 5 percent. Tipping taxi drivers is optional; a couple of euros will suffice.

TOILETS

The majority of museums and galleries have public toilets (monuments or historic sites always have some nearby). Bars, restaurants, cafés, department stores, airports, railway stations and car parks all have facilities.

Toilets may be labelled with a symbol of a man or a woman or the initials WC. Sometimes labels will be in Italian, but beware: *Uomini* is for men, *Donne* for women; however, *Signori* with a final 'i' is for men, but *Signore* with a final 'e' means women. Some facilities are unisex.

TOURIST INFORMATION

The **Italian National Tourist Board** (*Ente Nazionale Italiano per il Turismo*, abbreviated ENIT, <www.enit.it>) is represented in Italy and abroad. They publish detailed brochures with up-to-date information on accommodation, means of transport, general tips and useful addresses for tourists. ENIT has a number of international offices:

Australia and New Zealand: Italian Government Tourist Office, Level 4, 46 Market Street, NSW 2000 Sydney, Australia, tel: (02) 92621666.

Canada: Italian Government Tourist Board, Suite 907, South Tower, 175 Bloor Street East, Toronto, Ontario, M4W 3R8, tel: (416) 925 4882.

UK and Ireland: Italian State Tourist Board, 1 Princes Street, London W1B 2AY, tel: (020) 7408 1254.

US: Italian Government Tourist Board, Suite 1565, 630 Fifth Avenue, New York, NY 10111, tel: (212) 245 4822; Italian Government Tourist Board, Suite 2240, 500 North Michigan Avenue, Chicago, IL 60611, tel: (312) 644 0996/0; Italian Government Tourist Board, Suite 550, 12400 Wilshire Boulevard, Los Angeles, CA 90025, tel: (310) 820 1898.

The Tourist Board's main information office in **Rome** is at Via Parigi 5, tel: 06-488991 open Mon–Sat 9am–7pm. It operates kiosks at Stazione Termini in front of platform 4, open daily 8am–9pm, and at Fiumicino Airport (international arrivals, Terminal C), open daily 8am–9pm. A general tourist information Call Centre (tel: 06-82059127), with operators speaking Italian, English, French, Spanish and German, will answer any and all questions regarding tourism in Rome (open daily 9am–7.30pm). The council-run Chiama Roma service (Mon–Sat 4–7pm, toll-free tel: 060606; English speaking) provides tourist information round the clock.

There are also several tourist information points maintained by the city council dotted around the city and open daily from 9.30am–

7.30pm. These are at Castel Sant'Angelo–Piazza Pia; Fori Imperiali–Piazza del Tempio della Pace; Piazza delle Cinque Lune (Piazza Navona); Piazza Sonnino (Trastevere); Piazza San Giovanni in Laterano; Via dell'Olmata (Santa Maria Maggiore); Piazza dei Cinquecento (in front of the station); Via Nazionale (Palazzo delle Esposizioni); Via Minghetti (Fontana di Trevi).

Where's the nearest tourist office?	Dov'è l'ufficio turistico più vicino?

W

WEBSITES

A number of websites provide helpful information for tourists: <www.enit.it>, <www.romaturismo.com>, <www.abcroma.com>, <www.museidiroma.com>, <www.enjoyrome.com>, <www.whatsoninrome.com>.

For an affordable airfare to Rome, try <www.easyjet.com>, <www.ryanair.com> or <www.travelsupermarket.com>.

There is also a growing number of **internet cafés** situated in the centre of the city where you can check your email, surf the net and also have a coffee or drink. A centrally located internet café is Easy Everything at Via Barberini 2, <www.easyeverything.com>, which is open daily 8am–1am, has 250 PCs and some of the best rates in town.

Y

YOUTH HOSTELS *(Ostelli della Gioventù)*

Youth hostels are open to holders of membership cards issued by the International Youth Hostels Federation, or by the AIG *(Associazione Italiana Alberghi per la Gioventù)*.

Recommended Hotels

Italian hotels are classified by the government from one to five stars according to the facilities they offer. However, the star rating does not give a guide to the character or location of the hotel. Prices don't always include breakfast, so check this when you book. Inexpensive hotels are hard to find in Rome, so book early.

As a basic guide, we have used the symbols below to indicate high season prices per night for a double room with bath or shower, including service charge, tax and VAT. The hotels listed take major credit cards unless otherwise stated.

€€€€€	over 450 euros
€€€€	260–450 euros
€€€	140–260 euros
€€	70–140 euros
€	below 70 euros

PIAZZA NAVONA AND PANTHEON

Abruzzi €€€ *Piazza della Rotonda 69, 00186, tel: 06-97841351, fax: 06-69788076, <www.hotelabruzzi.it>*. Though recently refurbished, this remains one of the cheaper hotels in the city centre. Unique and dramatic direct views of the Pantheon are its strongest selling point; the rooms are simple but pleasant, and large for Rome. Prices go down in July and August.

Cesari €€€ *Via di Pietra 89a, 00186, tel: 06-6749701, fax: 06-67497030, <www.albergocesari.it>*. A pleasant, 18th-century hotel, but its past guests – Stendhal, Mazzini and Garibaldi – would not recognise the 1990s modernisation. Very central location. 47 rooms.

Grand Hotel de la Minerve €€€€€ *Piazza della Minerva 69, 00186, tel: 06-695201, fax: 06-6794165, <www.grandhoteldela minerve.com>*. This elegant 17th-century *palazzo* has provided comfortable lodging since Napoleonic times. Many of the tasteful contemporary rooms overlook Bernini's Piazza Minerva. 135 rooms.

Portoghesi €€€ *Via dei Portoghesi 1, 00186, tel: 06-6864231, fax: 06-6876976, <www.hotelportoghesiroma.com>*. Beat the devoted regulars and book early at this popular, reasonably priced, small hotel in a picturesque corner of Rome's Centro Storico. Modern bathrooms, air-conditioning, television and telephones are in each of the 27 comfortable, carpeted rooms. Mastercard and Visa only.

Raphael €€€€€ *Largo Febo 2, 00186, tel: 06-682831, fax: 06-6878993, <www.raphaelhotel.com>*. With a vine-draped façade, this intimate and refined establishment is decorated with antiques and works of art in the lobby and in many of the comfortable rooms. There is both a restaurant and bar in the hotel, but they're easy to overlook with Rome's loveliest piazza (Navona) a few steps away. Views from the terrace garden are hard to forget. Renowned American architect Richard Meier recently designed the hotel's ultra-modern third floor.

Sole Al Pantheon €€€€ *Piazza della Rotonda 63, 00186, tel: 06-6780441, fax: 06-69940689, <www.hotelsolealpantheon.com>*. An inn for 500 years, this refurbished boutique hotel retains all its charm while adding modern comforts and enjoying a superb location. Each of the 25 rooms is named after an illustrious guest of the distant past.

CAMPO DE' FIORI AND GHETTO

Arenula €€ *Via Santa Maria dei Calderari 47, 00186, tel: 06-6879454, fax: 06-6896188, <www.hotelarenula.com>*. A comfortable reasonably priced hotel, it's one of the few in the heart of the Jewish Ghetto and is within striking distance of many major sites. 50 rooms.

Pensione Barrett €€ *Largo di Torre Argentina 47, 00186, tel: 06-6868481, fax: 06-6892971, <www.pensionebarrett.com>*. Though small, with only 20 rooms, this hotel is comfortable and remarkably good value for money. It's also very central and only a five-minute stroll south of the Pantheon. No credit cards. Small extra charge for breakfast and air-conditioning.

Rinascimento €€€ *Via del Pellegrino 122, 00186, tel: 06-6874813, fax: 06-6833518, <www.hotelrinascimento.com>.* At the lower end of this price category, this pleasant family-run hotel has well-equipped, comfortable and characteristic, if slightly cramped, rooms. Ask for the room with a stunning view of the Chiesa Nuova.

Sole €€ *Via del Biscione 76, 00186, tel: 06-68806873, fax: 06-6893787, <www.solealbiscione.it>.* One of the few reasonably priced hotels in town, this one has individually decorated rooms that vary greatly. But you come here for the delightful terrace and the medieval neighbourhood, alive from early morning until late at night. 58 rooms. No credit cards. Parking spaces available for reasonable rates.

ROMAN FORUM AND COLOSSEUM

Capo d'Africa €€€€ *Via Capo d'Africa 54, 00184, tel: 06-772801, fax: 06-77280801, <www.hotelcapodafrica.com>.* A wonderfully peaceful boutique hotel. Behind the dramatic palm tree-lined entrance, its 64 rooms are warm yet very contemporary in design and feel. The views are delightful, and the Colosseum is only a five-minute walk away. Lower end of this price scale.

Edera €€€ *Via Poliziano 75, 00184, tel: 06-70453888, fax: 06-70453769, <www.leonardihotels.com>.* This is a quiet, unpretentious hotel with a small garden. Its rates are at the lower end of this price category. No restaurant. Parking spaces available. 51 rooms.

Forum €€€–€€€€ *Via Tor de' Conti 25, 00184, tel: 06-6792446, fax: 06-6786479, <www.hotelforumrome.com>.* An elegantly furnished hotel that has a spectacular view of the Imperial Forum from its delightful roof-garden restaurant, a perfect spot for both lunch and dinner. The Colosseum is a very short walk away. 80 rooms.

PIAZZA DI SPAGNA AND TRIDENTE

Condotti €€€ *Via Mario de' Fiori 37, 00187, tel: 06-6794661, fax: 06-6790457, <www.hotelcondotti.com>.* A quiet and comfortable hotel, it is in the very heart of Rome's most exclusive shopping district. Hotel pickings at relatively affordable prices are slim in this exclusive pedestrian-only area. 26 rooms.

Gregoriana €€€ *Via Gregoriana 18, 00187, tel: 06-6794269, fax: 06-6784258, <www.hotelgregoriana.it>*. In a very pleasant location at the top of the Spanish Steps, this converted and recently renovated convent has a distinctive art-deco style. Its pretty, comfortable rooms attract regular return guests, many in the fashion industry. 20 rooms.

Hassler Villa Medici €€€€€ *Piazza Trinità dei Monti 6, 00187, tel: 06-699340, fax: 06-6789991, <www.hotelhasslerroma.com>*. In a wonderful location overlooking the Spanish Steps and all of Rome, the family-owned Hassler has furnishings, house-proud service and a spectacular rooftop bar and restaurant to match. A few choice suites have remarkable terraces for the absolute splurge. 99 rooms. Wildly expensive but wildly luxurious.

Hotel Art €€€€ *Via Margutta 56, 00187, tel: 06-328711, fax: 06-36003995, <www.hotelart.it>*. Located in a former religious college, this hotel successfully blends the old and modern. Receptionists greet visitors from futuristic pods in what was once a chapel, with frescoed ceilings, stained-glass windows and a bar where the altar once stood. The rooms are on the small side but colourful and very comfortable. Views are of the arty Via Margutta's terracotta rooftops.

D'Inghilterra €€€€–€€€€€ *Via Bocca di Leone 14, 00187, tel: 06-699811, fax: 06-69922243, <www.royaldemeure.com>*. A perennial favourite sits amid the grid of top-of-the-line designer boutiques near the Spanish Steps. Antique furniture and a fine collection of Neapolitan gouaches preserve a distinct flavour of the past. Celebrity guests such as Ernest Hemingway, Mark Twain and Henry James found it a gem. 98 rooms.

Locarno €€€–€€€€ *Via della Penna 22, 00186, tel: 06-3610841, fax: 06-3215249, <www.hotellocarno.com>*. A centrally located hotel with an attractive vine-covered façade and art-nouveau interiors. Take breakfast in the lovely small outdoor courtyard, or walk two blocks to the Piazza del Popolo for a sunny alternative. 66 rooms.

Margutta €€–€€€ 3 *Via Laurina 34, 00187, tel: 06-3223674, fax: 06-3200395, <www.hotelmargutta.it>*. A small but centrally located hotel with eclectic decor, it attracts faithful return guests and offers reliable service. A few of the small rooms on the upper floor have their own terraces with views. 24 rooms.

De Russie €€€€€ *Via del Babuino 9, 00187, tel: 06-328881, fax: 06-32888888, <www.hotelderussie.it>*. *The* hotel in Rome. Since its opening in 2000 it has been consistently booked up, and is popular with the stars (George Clooney et al during the filming of *Ocean's Twelve*). Located in Rome's fashionable shopping district, with an atmospheric tiered garden, internal courtyard, and a fitness and spa centre, this hotel gets everything right. The rooms are plush, the staff are discreet but friendly, and the hotel's design is sleek and modern. Ask for a room with a view of Piazza del Popolo.

Scalinata di Spagna €€€–€€€€ *Piazza Trinità dei Monti 17, 00187, tel: 06-69940896, fax: 06-69940598, <www.hotelscalinata.com>*. The view over the city and down the Spanish Steps from this charming *pensione*-turned-up-market boutique hotel is fantastic. The rooms are modest for these rates, but they are always full nonetheless – location, location, location! WiFi access throughout. 16 rooms.

Suisse €€–€€€ *Via Gregoriana 54, 00187, tel: 06-6783649, fax: 06-6781258, <www.hotelsuisserome.com>*. This is a comfortable, efficiently family-run third-floor hotel in a good location near the Spanish Steps, where some hotels charge quadruple these rates. No fuss and very popular. 12 rooms.

VIA VENETO AND TREVI

Aleph €€€€–€€€€€ *Via di San Basilio 15, 00187, tel: 06-422 901, fax: 06-42290000, <www.boscolohotels.com>*. In this boutique hotel the lobby, bar, reading room and seafood restaurant are decorated in shades of fiery red, while the 96 bedrooms are inspired by

1930s and 1940s design. A popular top-floor bar and terrace opens in the summer months, and downstairs there is a lovely spa, with a mosaic Jacuzzi pool. Special deals online.

Eden €€€€€ *Via Ludovisi 49, 00187, tel: 06-478121, fax: 06-4821584, <www.hotel-eden.it>*. This hilltop luxury hotel with beautiful amenities has excellent views of the city from the famous rooftop terrace bar and restaurant. It's halfway between the Spanish Steps and the Via Veneto. 121 rooms.

Excelsior €€€€€ *Via Veneto 125, 00187, tel: 06-47081, fax: 06-4826205, <www.westin.com/excelsiorrome>*. The *grande dame* of the turn-of-the-20th-century hotels is extremely comfortable. It is adjacent to the US Embassy and a natural magnet for Americans and the Hollywood types who fill the sophisticated bar. 317 rooms.

Fontana €€€–€€€€ *Piazza di Trevi 96, 00187, tel: 06-6786113, fax: 06-6790024, <www.hotelfontana-trevi.com>*. A comfortable hotel housed in a converted monastery, it has smallish rooms but many of them have priceless views of the Trevi Fountain. Those without a view can repair to the roof garden and terrace. 25 rooms.

ST PETER'S AND THE VATICAN

Atlante Star €€€–€€€€ *Via Vitelleschi 34, 00193, tel: 06-6873233, fax: 06-6872300, <www.atlantehotels.com>*. Among the attractions offered here is the spectacular 360° view of St Peter's from its well-known and much respected roof-garden restaurant, Les Etoiles, and breathtaking views from many of the 85 rooms. The decor is a contemporary and the service is courteous, with lots of up-market attention to detail.

Columbus €€€–€€€€ *Via della Conciliazione 33, 00193, tel: 06-686 5435, fax: 06-6864874, <www.hotelcolumbus.net>*. This tastefully furnished four-star hotel is in a 15th-century palace built by Cardinal (and future Pope) Domenico della Rovere. There are original frescoes in the lobby and a fine restaurant. Three blocks from St Peter's Square, it has been a long-time favourite of visiting Vatican officials. 92 rooms.

AROUND TERMINI STATION

The Beehive €–€€ *Via Marghera 8, tel: 06-44704553, <www. the-beehive.com>*. A chic but very cheap option near Termini station, run by an American couple. The Beehive has a dorm room, apartments and private rooms decorated in a colourful and contemporary style, as well as a welcoming garden, a café for guests and highly knowledgeable staff.

Britannia €€€ *Via Napoli 64, 00184, tel: 06-4883153, fax: 06-48986316, <www.hotelbritannia.it>*. This comfortable hotel has a refined ambience and a variety of amenities, such as television, minibar, room safe and hair dryer, that make the price exceptionally fair. The convenient neighourhood is safe enough, but not very picturesque. 33 rooms.

Quirinale €€€€ *Via Nazionale 7, 00184, tel: 06-4707, fax: 06-4820099, <www.hotelquirinale.it>*. A large, efficiently run and well-decorated hotel just next door to the Teatro dell'Opera, the main reason for its popularity. Garden, outdoor dining in summer. 209 rooms.

Saint Regis Grand €€€€€ *Via Vittorio Emanuele Orlando 3, 00185, tel: 06-47091, fax: 06-4747307, <www.stregis.com>*. The Grand Hotel underwent a multi-million dollar face-lift in 1999. Stop by if only for afternoon tea, a year-round tradition, particularly in the winter. Better yet, check into one of Rome's most lavish (and pricey) guest rooms. 161 rooms.

FURTHER AFIELD

Cavalieri Hilton €€€€€ *Via A. Cadlolo 101, 00136, tel: 06-35091, fax: 06-35092241, <www.cavalieri-hilton.it>*. Set amid 6 hectares (15 acres) in a peaceful, but non-central location (15 minutes from the city centre), the hotel has splendid views of the residential neighbourhood of Monte Mario. Outdoor pool, terrace, park, tennis and arguably Rome's finest restaurant, renowned chef Heinz Beck's rooftop La Pergola. Excellent dining, indoors and alfresco. 370 rooms.

Recommended Restaurants

Authentic Roman cuisine has its basis in *la cucina povera*, the poor man's cooking. You will find these simple but delicious traditional dishes not only in most Roman *trattorie* but also in the most elegant and expensive restaurants. By law the nominal cover charge *(pane e coperto)* has been eliminated; it now seems to have been replaced by just a coperto or in some cases a service *(servizio)* charge. Note that around the national holiday of Ferragosto (15 August) many restaurants close for two, three, sometimes four weeks, as Romans head out of town. Restaurants also close for a week or so between Christmas and mid-January: it's best to call in advance during these periods. In January 2005 smoking was banned from restaurants, bars and cafés.

Roman restaurants serve lunch from 12.30 to 3pm and dinner from 8pm to 11pm. Some offer late-night supper and are open until 1 or 2am.

All restaurants listed here accept major credit cards unless otherwise stated. The price codes below are to give an idea of the cost of a three-course meal for two with a bottle of house wine and service included:

€€€€	over 70 euros
€€€	45–70 euros
€€	25–45 euros
€	below 25 euros

PIAZZA NAVONA AND PANTHEON

Da Baffetto € *Via del Governo Vecchio 114, tel: 06-6861617.* Open daily, 6.30pm–1am; not open for lunch. This pizzeria is a rowdy Roman institution, loved by all for the excellent pizza that comes straight from a wood-burning oven. The plain and simple *margherita* is everyone's favourite. They can't make them fast enough. No credit cards. No reservations – just join the queue outside if there is one.

Coco €€ *Piazza delle Coppelle 54, tel: 06-68136545, <www.coco restaurant.it>.* Lunch and dinner daily. A very varied menu that features the additional bonus (or not, depending on your point of view) of calorie and cholesterol counts for each dish. Choose from pizza, salads, meat and fish dishes, all of them good. The desserts are memorable, especially the hot chocolate cake. The setting is quite trendy.

Il Convivio Troiani €€€€ *Vicolo dei Soldati 31, tel: 06-6869432, <www.ilconviviotroiani.com>*. Dinner only; closed all day Sun. One of Rome's top restaurants, run by the three amiable Troiani brothers, with Angelo in the kitchen. Imaginative un-Roman dishes such as quail leg stuffed with foie gras, or minced cuttlefish with roasted peppers. Excellent fairly priced wine selection. Reservations recommended. Expect to pay about €100 or more a head.

Cul de Sac €–€€ *Piazza di Pasquino 73, tel: 06-68801094*. Lunch and dinner daily; open late. The oldest and one of the best-stocked wine bars in Rome. The space might be tight but the atmosphere and prices are just right. The array of cheeses, cold meats, Middle-Eastern-influenced snacks, hearty soups and salads are of consistently high quality. It gets packed, so be prepared to queue if you arrive at peak times (leave your name at the door as bookings cannot be taken).

Insalata Ricca € *Largo de' Chiavari, 85, tel: 06-68803656, <www.insalataricca.it>*. Lunch and dinner daily. Wide variety of large and freshly made salads are offered as well as a good selection of tasty pasta dishes. Claustrophobics won't enjoy the cosy seating. This is the original of a successful offspring.

Il Piccolo € *Via del Governo Vecchio 74, tel: 06-68801746*. Open daily, lunch and dinner. A lively and casual wine bar that offers a buffet serving a limited selection of traditional fare in a characteristic neighbourhood. Eat here before heading to the Piazza Navona for some street theatre.

La Rosetta €€€€ *Via della Rosetta 8, tel: 06-6861002, <www.larosetta.com>*. Lunch and dinner; closed Sun. Considered to be the best seafood restaurant in Rome, La Rosetta has next to no meat options. Fillet of sea bass with red wine sauce and artichokes is delicious. Imaginative use of spices and sauces. Selection of international wines. Reservations essential. Very expensive at dinner, cheaper for lunch.

Supperclub €€€ *Via de' Nari 14, tel: 06-68807207, <www.supper club.com>.* Dinner (and cocktails) only; open late. Located in an 18th-century palazzo, this trendy establishment is made up of a series of atmospherically lit rooms filled with huge sofas and cushions on which people eat. There's a hip fusion menu and live music or a DJ.

CAMPO DE' FIORI AND GHETTO

Crudo €€ *Via degli Specchi 6, tel: 06-6838989, <www.crudoroma. it>.* Lunch and dinner, closed Sun at dinner and Mon at lunch. The menu at Crudo ('raw' in English) is divided into delicate, medium and spiced, and the fish and meat served are raw, marinated or steamed. The 1960s decor, great wine list and buzzing bar make this a fun night out. Upper end of this price scale.

Ditirambo €€–€€€ *Piazza della Cancelleria 74, tel: 06-6871626, <www.ristoranteditirambo.it>.* Lunch and dinner, closed Mon for lunch. In this rustic and cosy space some imaginative combinations (such as ricotta flan served with sliced artichoke and a fruity pomegranate sauce) are served up to a cheerful and satisfied crowd of tourists and locals alongside traditional well-cooked cuts of meat and fish dishes. The pasta is home-made, as are the mouthwatering sweets, and the food is often made from organic ingredients. Many options for vegetarians. Visa only.

Il Pagliaccio €€€ *Via dei Banchi Vecchi 129, tel: 06-68809595, <www.ristoranteilpagliaccio.it>.* Lunch and dinner; closed Sun and Mon and Tues at lunch. A highly innovative and affordable top-class gourmet experience is to be had in this refined venue, courtesy of talented chef Anthony Genovese and pastry chef Marion Lichtle. Service is attentive and cordial, and there is an adventurous six-course taster menu for €75.

Del Pallaro € *Largo del Pallaro 15, tel: 06-68801488.* Lunch and dinner, closed Mon. This quintessentially Roman *trattoria* is a reliable favourite for big appetites and smaller budgets. There is no menu, but for about €20 (house wine and water included) you will be served several courses one after another and will leave feeling satisfyingly full. The fare is not particularly sophisticated, but is very tasty. The artichokes are excellent and the desserts home-made. The kitchen stays open until past midnight. No credit cards.

Piperno €€€ *Via Monte dei Cenci 9, tel: 06-68806629, <www.ristorantepiperno.it>.* Lunch and dinner; closed Mon all day and Sun for dinner. Opened in 1856, this longtime favourite in the heart of the Ghetto serves Roman-Jewish specialities, such as *carciofi alla giudia* (fried whole artichokes) and Jerusalem artichokes in a number of delicious variations, as well as fish, veal and pasta dishes. Reservations are recommended.

Al Pompiere €€–€€€ *Via S. Maria de' Calderari 38, tel: 06-6868377.* Lunch and dinner; closed Sun. Waistcoated and greying waiters serve diners in the frescoed rooms of this first floor restaurant located in the picturesque Palazzo Cenci. The dishes are Roman and Roman-Jewish and include some ancient Roman offerings. The standard is consistently good.

Trattoria Moderna €€ *Vicolo dei Chiodaroli 16, tel: 06-68803423, <www.trattoriamoderna.it>.* Lunch and dinner; closed Sun. A relative newcomer to the city's restaurant scene, Trattoria Moderna has an appealing modern decor of earthy tones. The owners are experienced Roman restaurateurs and the menu is accordingly classical Mediterranean, but with some successful modern touches.

COLOSSEUM

Luzzi €–€€ *Via Celimontana 1, tel: 06-7096332.* Lunch and dinner; closed Wed. A very popular neighbourhood *trattoria* just a short walk away from the Colosseum. Luzzi is loud and cheerful and serves up good pizzas, pasta dishes and simple second courses of fish and meat. Outdoor seating.

GiNa €–€€ *Via San Sebastianello 7/a, tel: 06-6780251, <www.gina roma.com>.* Mon–Sat lunch and dinner, Sun closes 8pm. In an almost all-white and funky setting, this is a good place to come for lunch, a light dinner or drinks. The menu features lots of salads, sandwiches, soups and pasta dishes. Wine is available by the glass or bottle.

'Gusto €–€€€ *Piazza Augusto Imperatore 9, tel: 06-3226273, <www.gusto.it>.* Lunch and dinner daily. 'Gusto has a pizzeria downstairs, an up-market restaurant upstairs, and a wine bar with excellent wines and a great selection of snacks and cheeses on the other side in Via della Frezza. There's also an *osteria* next to that (at Via della Frezza 16). The quality is always high, service is fast and there is a large porticoed outdoor seating area most of the year round.

Naturist Club € *Via della Vite 14, tel: 06-6792509.* Lunch and dinner; closed Sat at lunch and all day Sun. Don't be put off by the name – it's an historic Rome macrobiotic restaurant, tucked away on the fourth floor of this palazzo. At lunchtime it operates as a self-service vegetarian restaurant, by night you can eat à la carte (including fish dishes) or from a fixed menu accompanied by organic wines.

Nino €€–€€€ *Via Borgognona 11, tel: 06-6795676.* Lunch and dinner; closed Sun. Good traditional Tuscan food and Chianti wine selections have been long favoured by the shopowners and patrons of this chic neighbourhood. Nino is reasonably priced for such an expensive area.

Obikà €–€€ *Via dei Prefetti 26/a, tel: 06-6832630, <www.obika. it>.* Lunch and dinner daily. Touting itself as the first (and so far only) 'mozzarella bar' in Rome, this minimal venue pays homage to the delicious cheese that is delivered daily from the neighbouring Campania region. Customers can eat it sushi-style at counters or in a variety of dishes in the elegant restaurant section. There are plenty of options for non-cheese eaters, scrumptious desserts too and a very affordable lunch menu.

VIA VENETO AND TREVI FOUNTAIN

Cantina Cantarini €€ *Piazza Sallustio 12*, tel: 06-485528. Lunch and dinner; closed Sun. In a smart neighbourhood this is a high-quality, family-run *trattoria* where the price is still right. The dishes are Roman, with influences from the Marches, and are meat-based the first part of the week and fish-based from Thursday at dinner to Saturday.

Nanà €€ *Via della Panetteria 37*, tel: 06-69190750. Lunch and dinner; closed Mon. Situated a short walk from Trevi Fountain, this restaurant is a real find in a generally overpriced and low-quality tourist area. The decor is chic and rustic, the staff friendly and the food influenced by southern Italy, with speciality dishes from the Calabria, Sicilia and Puglia regions.

VATICAN AND PRATI

L'Arcangelo €€€ *Via G.G. Belli 59–61*, tel: 06-3210992. Lunch and dinner; closed Sat lunch and Sun. The prints on the walls and linen tablecloths form an unexpected backdrop to some very imaginative culinary offerings and an understated gourmet experience. There's a resonably priced taster menu of Roman cuisine. Lower end of this price scale.

Le Pain à Table €–€€ *Via delle Milizie 13/corner Via Oltranto 57*, tel: 06-37500580. Breakfast, lunch and dinner Mon–Sat; open from 5.30pm Sun). A French-style café and bakery where you can have your *pain au chocolat* and cappuccino in the morning, soups, salads and light fare at midday, and creative cuisine in the evening. Also highly recommended is brunch, which includes impressive salads and savory *crostini*.

Del Frate €€ *Via degli Scipioni 118*, tel: 06-3236437. Lunch and dinner; closed Sun at lunch. This chic little *enoteca* is filled with interesting bottles of wine for sale or to be sampled by the glass. As you do so, you can nibble appetisers or enjoy a range of hot and cold and very tasty dishes.

TRASTEVERE AND TESTACCIO

Alberto Ciarla €€€€ *Piazza San Cosimato 40, tel: 06-5818668, <www.albertociarla.com>.* Dinner only; closed Sun. Recommended for elegant seafood and fish dishes, and worth a visit for the iced-fish display alone. Outdoor dining is available. Stroll about after dinner to take a look at this colourful neighbourhood. Reservations recommended.

Checchino dal 1887 €€€ *Via di Monte Testaccio 30, tel: 06-5743816, <www.checchino-dal-1887.com>.* Lunch and dinner; closed Sun and Mon. An acclaimed first-rate *trattoria* serving a traditional cuisine based on the cheap cuts and offal from Testaccio's slaughterhouse. Tripe, brains, liver, sweetbreads and intestines are loved by Romans but there's much else to keep more conservative palates happy. Reserve for dinner.

Glass Hostaria €€–€€€ *Vicolo del Cinque 58, tel: 06-58335903.* Open dinner only; closed Mon. Excellent taster menus, home-made bread and creative dishes such as *tagliolini al nero di seppia con capesante, zucchine e pomodorini* (black squid ink pasta with scallops, courgettes and small tomatoes) and *tortelli verdi di trota e ortica con pomodoro fresco* (trout and nettle tortelli served with fresh tomato) make this restaurant in Trastevere a memorable experience.

Paris €€–€€€ *Piazza San Callisto 7a, tel: 06-5815378.* Lunch and dinner; closed Mon all day and Sun for dinner. On offer at this delightful restaurant (not Parisian at all) are a delightful baroque dining room and a terrace for summertime dinners. A creative selection of both fish and meat dishes.

AROUND TERMINI STATION

Agata e Romeo €€€€ *Via Carlo Alberto 45, tel: 06-4466115; <www.agataeromeo.it>.* Lunch and dinner; closed Sat and Sun. This restaurant, managed by *sommelier* Romeo together with his wife Agata (the chef) and their daughter, is considered to be one of the best in Rome. Traditional dishes have a fresh twist and desserts are to die for, including white peach mousse with almond ice cream and dark chocolate fondant with raspberry sauce. Reservations essential.

Trimani Wine Bar €€ *Via Cernaia 37b, tel: 06-4469630.* Open all day; closed Sun. An excellent choice of wines (the Trimani family first became famous for their nearby wine store) and good food is found in an elegant and friendly atmosphere. Sample a number of good-to-excellent wines by the glass accompanied by a light or full meal at reasonable prices.

Vivendo €€€ *Via V.E. Orlando 3, tel: 06-47092736.* Lunch and dinner; closed Sat at lunch and Sun. Sophisticated cuisine in the luxurious dining rooms of the St Regis Grand Hotel. The menu is international, but heavily slanted towards the innovative Mediterranean. There are affordable *menu degustazione* (tasting menus) too.

FURTHER AFIELD IN ROME

Cecilia Metella €€ *Via Appia Antica 125–129, tel: 06-5136743.* Lunch and dinner; closed Mon. Pleasant, with an ample garden, near the Roman tomb of Cecilia Metella. Especially popular for celebrations and the traditional Sunday afternoon exodus when it fills with families. Roman cuisine. Upper end of this price scale.

La Pergola dell'Hotel Hilton €€€€ *Via Cadlolo 101, tel: 06-35092152.* Dinner only; closed Sun and Mon. This elegant penthouse restaurant with three Michelin stars has a spectacular view overlooking the city and Roman hills, and an acclaimed chef who creates superb Mediterranean dishes. Reservations essential. Average price €130 or more.

Uno e Bino €€–€€€ *Via degli Equi 58, tel: 06-4460702.* Dinner only, closed Mon. An intimate but unassuming-looking restaurant in Rome's student district, San Lorenzo, just east of the station, this actually offers an outstanding gourmet experience. From audacious combinations and choice of ingredients to food presentation and the extensive wine list served by knowledgeable staff, this is very good value. Visa and Diners Club only.

INDEX

Berlitz pocket guide

Rome

Fourteenth Edition 2008

Written by Patricia Schultz
Updated by Annie Shapero
Principal photographer: Anna Mockford and Nick Bonnetti
Edited by Alex Knights
Series Editor: Tony Halliday

All Rights Reserved
© 2008 Berlitz Publishing/Apa Publications GmbH & Co. Verlag KG, Singapore Branch, Singapore

Printed in Singapore by Insight Print Services (Pte) Ltd, 38 Joo Koon Road, Singapore 628990. Tel: (65) 6865-1600. Fax: (65) 6861-6438

Berlitz Trademark Reg. U.S. Patent Office and other countries. Marca Registrada

Photography credits
All photography by Anna Mockford and Nick Bonnetti except for Jon Arnold Images/Alamy 78; Bridgeman Art Library 78; Chris Coe 9, 15, 24, 65, 99; Frances Gransden 27, 33, 55; Tony Halliday 22, 53, 60, 70; Italian National Tourist Board 100; Alex Knights 14; Tina Lee 18; David Sanger Photography/Alamy 26; Alessandra Santarelli 88, 89; STR/AFP/Getty Images 20; Museums and Galleries, Vatican City, Rome 68; Daniel Vittet 3TR; Bill Wassman 2B, 11, 13, 28, 35, 43, 58, 59, 63, 64, 72, 80, 83, 84, 91, 92

Cover picture: JLI Images/Alamy

Contact us

At Berlitz we strive to keep our guides as accurate and up to date as possible, but if you find anything that has changed, or if you have any suggestions on ways to improve this guide, then we would be delighted to hear from you.

Berlitz Publishing, PO Box 7910, London SE1 1WE, England.
fax: (44) 20 7403 0290
email: berlitz@apaguide.co.uk
www.berlitzpublishing.com